WOMAN AT THE
EDGE OF TWO WORLDS
WORKBOOK

WOMAN AT THE EDGE OF TWO WORLDS
WORKBOOK

MENOPAUSE AND THE FEMININE RITES OF PASSAGE

EXERCISES, MEDITATIONS, AND CEREMONIES
FOR TRANSFORMATION AND JOY

LYNN V. ANDREWS

HarperPerennial
A Division of HarperCollinsPublishers

HarperCollins books may be purchased for educational, business, or sales promotional use. For information please write: Special Markets Department, HarperCollins Publishers, Inc., 10 East 53rd Street, New York, NY 10022.

FIRST EDITION

Designed by Jessica Shatan

Illustrations by Ginny Joyner

ISBN 0-06-095064-1

94 95 96 97 98 ❖/CW 10 9 8 7 6 5 4 3 2 1

⟡ ACKNOWLEDGMENTS ⟡

I would like to acknowledge my tireless agent, Al Lowman, and thank my editor at HarperCollins, Janet Goldstein, for her encouragement and insight on this project.

Thank you so much also to Kathy Duckworth for her dedication to my work.

✦ CONTENTS ✦

FREEDOM:
FINDING THE INNER TRUTH THAT SETS YOU FREE

CELEBRATION:
TAKING STOCK OF WHAT YOU HAVE BECOME
AND REINVENTING YOUR VISION OF LIFE

A Prayer for Balance

Oh, Great Mother, As I look out across the desert,
Green from rain,
And the mountains in the distance,
I ask that you give me guidance along my path of heart,
I ask that you help me to understand my powers of creativity.

As the clouds above me cast shadows on the desert floor, I know that
    I have often lost my way,
And when the shadow aspects of myself diminish my life,
I become afraid.

Oh, Great Mother, Take my hand,
Help me to see the trail
So that I may find my way home.

I am often tired these days. I think sometimes that I will be bereft of
    balance forever,
That there is no one to help me.

But as I look at the great mountains in the distance, As their
    silhouette is etched against the sky
With such clarity,
I know that somewhere in my heart
I have known such clarity before,
And that you are there for me.
It is only me that sometimes refuses to see you.

And I will open my eyes now, And I will see your face,
Just as the sunlight bursting through the clouds
Illuminates the flowers all around me.
I will begin to shine as they do.

I am flowering for you, Great Mother. I am lending my beauty to the
    universe for a short time.
And I realize that this life is a process
Of seed and stalk and growth and flowering,
And then death.

But death is only a rebirth back into spirit, a rebirth back into life.
And you may call me anytime, Great Spirit,
Back into your arms.
So I am here for you, Great Mother,
I am here for you, Great Spirit,
I am like a hollow log
With your love and your energy flowing through me
Forever.

Help me to walk in beauty and power All the days of my life.
Ho.

✦ PREFACE ✦

So many times in life when I have a spiritual journey, a spiritual idea, a truth that I am trying to share, I sit and I talk to a gathering of students, and they hear the wisdom, but how do they make that wisdom part of their own dream? I have found that wisdom becomes part of your personal domain through some aspect of experience. Often that experience can be found through story. In *Woman at the Edge of Two Worlds* I take women on my journey into menopause and describe how I took four of my apprentices to meet Woman at the Edge of Two Worlds, the great goddess who stands at that gateway and initiates women proudly and with great celebration into elder life. She initiates you not as a preparation for death, but in preparation for a newly recovered life and all the wisdom and power that that means.

Woman at the Edge of Two Worlds Workbook facilitates many of the ceremonies and experiences that I describe in my book *Woman at the Edge of Two Worlds*. It enables you, as a woman, to deal with the four positions on the sacred wheel of life: your physicalness, your substance of life in the south; your emotional nature, your dream life, your place of transformation in the west; your spirit and your health as an adult in the north; and your mental and intellectual capabilities, your abilities to rationalize and to see things in a larger picture in the east. All of these aspects are included within this workbook to bring you to a new position of power, balance, and understanding. If you move through each of the meditations, visualizations, and creative activities you will, by the end of the book, see very clearly who you are and how proud you can be of the woman that you have become.

I work with all different aspects and passages that a woman goes through in a lifetime, because I don't believe that you can isolate one passage from another. You will find as you move through these exercises that there may be places within yourself that are more stressed, that feel more trauma than you ever imagined. You may find those places within yourself around puberty, childbirth, or feelings that you never realized even existed, for instance, emotions around having children or not having children. Whatever your path has been, when you find those places of trauma within yourself, you need to take a look at each of the choices you have made in your life and make sure that you are clear about those choices. These meditations are designed to go very deeply into your psyche and into your emotional nature so that at last you can finally let go of old baggage that no longer serves you. As you move to the end of this workbook you will find that there is an aspect of creativity and freedom that you will begin to experience that you have never, perhaps, found before.

As an author, and shaman healer, I have seen the people I have apprenticed over the years learn to work through various aspects of their childhood conditioning, processes of addiction, disharmony in their lives. They learn to resonate with the rhythms of nature, and pieces of confusion drop away and they begin to celebrate who they really are, not just who the world wants them to be. They begin to find a wellspring of creativity and power that was always with them

but they just never saw.

Part of what you experience in the gateway of wise-blood and menopause is the rejuvenation of your point of view and your vision in this lifetime, and with that comes a new kindling of the fires of creativity. I am mentioning this to you, because if you look for it, you will begin to see it even sooner, and perhaps you will be able to manifest that creative impulse into something very real. You have accomplished much in your life. You have seen much. You have been down many trails, not just one, and as a woman standing at the edge of two worlds, this is a chance now to make those choices for yourself, for your own fulfillment, for your own wisdom, and for your own extraordinary creativity on any level that you choose.

✦ ENTERING THE GATEWAYS ✦

Several years ago I began my journey through the feminine rites of passage with my teachers in the Sisterhood of the Shields. They began our ceremonies by taking me to a cave in the mountains of Canada. This ancient cave has been used for initiation for thousands of years. Many of the petroglyphs on its walls have been carbondated to several thousand years before Christ. In this cave I first experienced the real importance of initiation for women's passages into different levels of life. I say "different levels of life," because I think that with each passage there is a new plateau that should be recognized as a time, not only of sacred ceremony, but also a time of taking stock and silent introspection. At each plateau your accomplishments in life can be celebrated. They may not be accomplishments that are recognized in the world as something special, but each accomplishment of life, whether it is raising children, being married or divorced, going into puberty, or moving through the gateways of wise-blood, or menopause, is a true accomplishment on a very personal and unique level within each of us.

As the Sisterhood of the Shields rolled aside the giant boulder that has held this cave of initiation secret for so many centuries, we performed a short circle ceremony of cleansing where we picked up a fire stick and cleansed our bodies of negativity. Then my teachers,

Agnes Whistling Elk and Ruby Plenty Chiefs, took me down into this cave that was very, very dark. Agnes led the way, and I followed in her footsteps with Ruby Plenty Chiefs picking up the trail. To be in this cave in the wilderness was an extraordinary experience—to hear the soundlessness of the granite walls, to feel the radiance in the darkness. I felt the memory of other women who had walked before me and done ceremony just as I. As we came to each niche along the cave wall, Agnes would light a candle that was set there for us.

Finally, after walking in a spiraling fashion down and down toward the heart of Mother Earth, we came to a large cavern. It was within this cavern that I sat with my teachers, talking with them over the ancient mother gourd about the teachings of the sacred wheel and the gourd mysteries and what that meant to all women. These teachings were not only secret and sacred and only for our ceremonies, but these teachings also had to do with every woman's expression in life, of her truth and her spirit. They were about balance—about balancing each of the four directions on the sacred wheel. The reason we use the sacred wheel is because it's a paradigm for the process of mind. It gives us a form within which we can begin to see our reality as a totality in life, not just an isolated incident. In other words, when women are moving through puberty, they so often isolate that experience from childbirth, from menopause, never looking forward to the next experience as part of the ceremony that they are performing presently. Therefore, I bring to you some of these teachings so that you can begin to use them in your life.

I realized, when we were sitting in this ancient cave of initiation, that oftentimes so much of what we do in our social structure eliminates even the thought of spirituality or sacredness in terms of enlightenment, where you are moving toward a true balance of wisdom. It is as if spirituality makes you less credible in a professional sense. It was in this cave, feeling the luminosity of the darkness, of the sound of our voices echoing against the ancient walls as the voices of other women had echoed for so many centuries, that I felt the presence of those other women. I felt the Sisterhood and the support of other women surrounding us. As they lent their support to us, I felt that we were lending back that energy in like kind, so that the experience could become a circle of friendship, of celebrating the differences and similarities that all of us have. I realized as we sat there in that ancient cavern that these teachings needed to be celebrated in our society today so that women could understand how precious, how beautiful, and how unique they truly are.

It is so easy for me to lecture to you about the truths that I have learned and have been gifted with, but how do you make those gifts part of your own dream? Because of that, I want to lead you along a path and exercise certain aspects within your brain, within your heart, that perhaps you haven't touched in a long time, so that the chance for something new can happen within you. Part of the unknowable and unnameable, those aspects of power that are part of the mystery and the magic of life, can speak to you, possibly for the first time. It is with great joy and excitement that I can share these mysteries with you.

There is a beauty and a power and a balance within each of us, but so few of us seem to know how to access that aesthetic and present it into our lives as part of our wholeness. These teachings are about health. They are about balance between the physical and the spiritual. For all of the spiritual work you do, you have to stay strong physically. How do you find those hidden trails of comfort and balance within your own soul? The answers are already waiting for you, but you can't quite seem to see them. You have a sense that there is a knowing within your own being, but you don't always know how to welcome that knowing into a language that you understand. This work is about that. It is about finding the heartland within your own spirit, that place that is magical and free and full of a kind of wildness, an instinctual nature that can express itself without guilt, without fear. That's what we're trying to do here. We're trying to communicate on levels that, perhaps, you haven't experienced before. And within that communication come a purity and a beauty that are the essential you.

Thank you and blessings on your path of heart.

✧ HOW TO USE THIS BOOK ✧

This is a workbook that was designed around the teachings of the sacred gourd. These teachings were given to me by the shaman society of women called the Sisterhood of the Shields when I entered into the gateway of wise-blood, or menopause. The gourd symbolically represents the wombness of all women and becomes the "new womb" for seeding and creating the magic in your second life. The sacred gourd teachings are many and include some aspects that perhaps you are not familiar with. All of the things that you will need for working with the gourd are included in the chapter How to Make Your Gourd: Opening the Womb of Creativity. A gourd can be purchased at a market, at a gourd farm, at many places that carry vegetables and fruits. It can be any kind of gourd, but it needs to be a gourd that speaks to you. Every gourd is different, and when you move yourself into that place of listening and spirituality within your being, you will see almost immediately that the gourd has a very special secret message for you. It represents the womb of the universe and the womb in each woman.

The making of the gourd is an important part of this workbook. If you choose not to make the gourd, then you may simply want to read this book for information, for meditation purposes. It is also a wonderful book to experience with other women in ceremony, in circle. It is also an excellent workbook to share with your family, because as you move through the gateway of menopause, it is important for other people in your life who are close to you to understand what you are going through and to celebrate with you. This is a passage that somehow needs to be honored, not hidden or feared. *Woman at the Edge of Two Worlds Workbook* gives women tools for self-expression, new ways of taking their intangible feelings out of themselves and forming them into reality. One of those ways is by creating the Changing Woman Doll. It is constructed out of your fears, your wisdom, your old undealt-with conditioning, and baggage from the history in your family that needs to, perhaps, be left behind. This process helps you form a fresh point of view.

A lot of the text of this book is written as a meditation so you can experience the ideas more deeply if you choose. Meditations allow you to set aside your everyday life and problems of the mind and heart and drop into new experiences and untraveled dimensions. I have put these meditations on tape with beautiful music. They are available to you if you call my number at the back of this book. Another way that you can use these meditations is to speak them onto a tape yourself or just read these meditations in the quietness of your own life. These meditations have been written as a tapestry of sound and words. Each meditation or visualization works with your heart, your mind, and your spirit in the various aspects of the four directions. The four directions represent a paradigm for the process of mind, so they represent physicalness in the south, trust and innocence of the child. In the west is your adolescent self, emotions, the sacred dream, death and rebirth, transformation. In the north is symbolically represented the adult, strength, and spirit. In the east is represented the old wise one, mind, illumination. The four directions

represent a way of seeing yourself in life and a way of approaching
life with a tangible and visible perception of meaning. As you grow,
the visualizations also expand. New knowledge will be revealed to
you as you repeat them again and again throughout your evolution-
ary process.

This book also serves as a journal for you. The book itself invites
you to write in it from beginning to end. It is very important to use
the worksheets as you proceed so you have a complete journal of discovery when you finish. This book will be of great use to you as you
help other sisters along their path and in your future. It will help you
to chart your progress and your development as you create the new
woman of power that is you—reborn and redefined through the gateway of menopause. If you have a daughter, it could be a wonderful
gift for her in later years.

As I have said many times in my work, one day, perhaps, you will
want to set aside your personal history and step fully and completely into the unknown mysteries of power. I talk about a power
animal, a dreaming power animal, in this book. The dreaming
power animal has to do with the essence of your nature, oftentimes,
the essence of a denied or unexpressed nature within you that is
wild and yet, wise. This dreaming power animal is a protection for
you and helps guide you down uncharted paths that you have never
walked on before. I ask you to do this dreaming power animal with
a partner, because so often when we have discoveries of spirit
within our lives we are afraid to share them or we hold them close
to us as a very sacred treasure, in a sense, almost unwilling to share
them. I hope you will find that menopause is actually the beginning
of true sisterhood, and the dreaming power animal meditation and

dancing it awakes will help you to begin down that road if it is unfamiliar to you.

It is helpful when doing some of these mediations and work with the gourds to have a place in mind, a place in the wilderness where you can work and dream that is unspoiled, maybe that has ancient trees still growing, cactuses that are hundreds of years old, the eternal ocean, someplace where the light of the sun and the moon can be experienced to its fullest.

Gourd Woman is a guide who you will meet during the course of your reading, and she is a guardian and a guide to the mysteries of the sacred gourd. Many of these mysteries will come to you in the form of dreams or as experiences and interactions that you will have not only as you are reading the book itself but also with your women friends in the years to come. This book is designed to reach you on very deep levels and to comfort you along your way.

The sections of this workbook are titled Fear, Hope, Freedom, and Celebration. Remember that as you journey you might think, "Oh, I have no fear. That is something that doesn't relate to me. I'll just skip over this part." Please move through each of the aspects. Oftentimes, the smarter you are, the better you fool yourself. There will be aspects within your own nature that you have hidden even from yourself. As you move through these sections, you will find pages on which you can write and questions that I have formulated for you. You may also want to ask your own questions and write them down.

The only other thing that you need with this workbook is a dedication to your own truth, health, and sense of well-being. Hopefully, part of what I bring to you in my workbooks is a new way of Seeing. I want you to see not only what happens around you in your daily life, but also the patterns and flow of energy that create these daily

events. These exercises and meditations will give you the opportunity
to exercise "muscles" that you, perhaps, do not know that you have.

When you are working in the meditative state, use your power and intent as best you can. Oftentimes, my apprentices will tell me that when they first meditate, they drop into an almost trance-like sleep. If you are working with a partner and this occurs, be sure to let your partner know what is happening to you so you can repeat the visualization another time. If you have real difficulty with falling asleep during the meditations, you may want to sit up during them. Sometimes it is good for someone to fall asleep. This sometimes happens because the conscious mind needs to be at rest so that the information can slip directly into the subconscious. On the whole, however, I would rather that you stay awake and be fully aware, because it is important that you begin to work on your true process of Seeing. It is important that you feel the shift of moods and emotions within these meditations, because an essential element of ceremony is always emotion—feelings of power and excitement, exultation, sadness, and love. All of these emotions help you to discover and empower your will, and also your shaman will—your energy center around your navel. It may be that shamanism is something that you are not interested in or have not ever heard of, but shamanism is really a word that describes the uses and understanding of energy, the energy field within your own body, the energies of all living things.

We as human beings can learn to choreograph the energies of this universe. Knowingly or unknowingly, it is through your will and intent that creativity and healing energy is produced in the world. If you use only your mind and not your emotions and your heart, you will certainly never be a shaman and you will never be a wise woman of power.

So open your heart and mind to all of the new possibilities that await you during this extraordinary journey of menopause. Use the tools for comforting your heart and transforming your spirit. Experience the different plateaus that you come to as deeply as you can. Use the diary to write in. Make your Changing Woman Doll and your gourd with your whole heart and soul. Put yourself into this book and it will give you so much in return. This workbook is a process and it can take as long as you want or you can do it as quickly as you want. It is up to you. You are the prime mover in this process called your life.

FEAR

LETTING GO OF CONFUSION AND FEAR

RELEASE

Anytime you are possessed by an emotion that you cannot control, know that it does not belong to you. Imagine that the negative emotion is muddy water pouring down through your hands, legs, and feet and into the earth. Or take that emotion into your hands and release it like a hawk—let it fly away. We tend to hold on to fears and negative energy in an addictive way. Release your fears and let power come into you. Create a welcoming void within, through the power of release. Release is one of the most important acts that you can learn on your path to power.

—The Power Deck

WANDERING WITH INTENT

LIVING LIKE AN ARROW, NOT LIKE A TARGET

✧ ✧ ✧ ✧ ✧ ✧ ✧ ✧ ✧ ✧ ✧ ✧ ✧ ✧ ✧ ✧ ✧

Introduction

The feminine rites of passage are ceremonies that originate from the teachings of the sacred gourd and have many different aspects. These aspects can be placed around the sacred wheel in the four directions. Working with the actual gourd is how you begin to understand your own feminine energy, or wombness, and helps you to understand yourself and your passages through life.

One aspect of the sacred wheel is the finding of the gourd in the south and the physical making of the gourd in the form of a rattle, in the form of a talking bowl, in the form of the sacred womb.

In the west of the sacred wheel you look at the gourd from the aspect of life and death, from the aspect of the sacred dream and how this gourd enables you to dream and helps you move into the sacred dreamtime and other dimensions of reality other than the everyday physical reality that we know and that is familiar.

If you take the gourd to the north position on the wheel, you look at the gourd from the place of prayer. How does the gourd enable you to pray, to move into that place of strength and wisdom and spirit within your own being, and assist you in becoming more powerful, more capable of healing not only those around you in the world but also and of course, firstly, yourself? To heal this planet we must always heal ourselves first.

In the east of the sacred wheel the gourd enables you, as an apprentice to the spirit, as an apprentice to higher consciousness and shamanism, to look at many aspects of yourself that perhaps you don't usually look at—that place within yourself that is the trickster. Even when taking yourself seriously, this is the place of playfulness and of openness to things that are new.

A big problem in our society and something that I talk about a great deal is the inability of people to let go of their old baggage, their old stuff, their old ideas, and be open to something new—not necessarily to believe in it or not believe in it, but to be open. Life is a dialectic between positive and negative poles of energy, which implies opposites and flow between opposites.

In the east on the wheel there is one aspect of the teaching of the sacred gourd that has to do with openness. Because the east position is directly across the wheel from the west, it also brings into play aspects of the west at the same time. For instance, how do you experience the sacred void? What in fact do those words mean to you? Is it just an intellectual exercise when I say "the sacred void"? Does a womb come up in your mind? Do you think of the Grand Canyon? Do you think of a valley? Do you think of a place of receiving like a basket, and what does that basket receive? Does it receive energy? What form do those energy particles take in your mind and in your heart? Do you think of an empty gourd?

Ceremony/Meditation

For a moment I would like you to think of those words, *sacred void*. Move into your body mind. Take your consciousness down from your intellect in your head, down into the area of shaman power around your navel. Collect your thoughts around your navel and begin to form your intent around this concept of sacred void. Allow yourself to come up with a vision, something that you sense, a quality of openness that we call the sacred void.

I'll give you several minutes.

Take a deep breath. Now that you have sensed—this doesn't necessarily mean that you have to see—a sacred void or a form for that void, you have a sense of it, perhaps, better now than you did before, an opening within yourself or even within the world that surrounds you.

Now I'd like you to think for a moment about the word *openness* and what that means to you. I'd like you to bring your consciousness now up into your heart. Have the experience for a few moments of opening your heart. Visualize a beautiful emerald green light around your chest. Take a deep breath and feel your heart begin to expand and open as you move yourself into the center of my words. Take another deep breath and feel your heart becoming warmer. Let those feelings go deeply into the sense of who you are, allowing yourself to expand and expand. See the green light, at first hovering around your body closely. Then see that green light expanding first a foot, then two feet, then three feet around your body. Take a deep breath and expand again. See that green light now filling the entire room, knowing that the source of that light is the expanded nature of your own heart.

Often, when we think of opening our hearts in daily life, we become afraid. When you open your heart, anything can come in. Good can come in, and sometimes things that are not so good. So we close up our hearts and we say, "Well, I'll just open it up a little bit today, but I'm going to be careful, because I don't want to be hurt."

I'd like you to think for a moment of what is left out of your experience in your daily life. Let's assume that if your heart is closed, you do keep out certain aspects of pain. What I'd like you to do right now is to describe to yourself four things, like new relationships and new experiences, that are positive that are kept out of your heart space when it is contracted.

Take several minutes to think of four things, good things, that are kept away from your personal experience when your heart is closed.

I'll give you some time.

Now that you have thought of four things that you keep out of your heart, good things, if your heart is closed, I'd like you, for a few moments while we are praying and working here together, to just allow your heart to open. Imagine what it would be like to allow yourself to just love without conditions, without judging. Allow yourself to feel that experience.

I'll give you some moments.

The ability to open and to close one's emotions, one's ideas, one's heart, one's mind, is a great gift, because we can at will allow ourselves to experience all of the magnificence of life, but only if we understand how to become receptive instead of afraid.

I'd like you to take another deep breath and imagine that you are walking in a wilderness desert. There are beautiful saguaro cactuses reaching up toward the cobalt blue sky. There are beautiful boulders and rock mountains surrounding you. There is chaparral and tamarisk trees and olive trees, their branches brushing the desert floor. You are walking along a dry creek bed. It is cool. It is springtime. There are wildflowers everywhere, blue and yellow, red and white. Birds are chirping. There is a gentle breeze against your skin.

You are wandering in the desert and you feel very loose in your body. You feel no tension in your mind or in your muscles, and you are wandering aimlessly. At first that is a very pleasant feeling, but then as the sun goes toward the horizon and it becomes cooler out, long slanted shadows cross your path as you walk. You begin to get colder, and your stomach is growling and you're hungry. You're still wandering aimlessly. You have no path. You have no mountain to climb. You have no home. You have no responsibility. You are simply a wanderer in the wilderness of life. When the wind blows, you go one way, and when the wind blows from another direction, you go the other way.

You see a tree with fruit up ahead. You pick an orange and it tastes good. Then you wander on down another trail. Maybe there is something to eat down that trail and maybe there isn't. Maybe there is no food for you for a long time. You don't know where to place your effort, and when you come to a trail that forks in two different directions, you don't know which way to go. And you wander off again into the wilderness.

You let that image slowly fade away, and you think to yourself, "That's a kind of openness. That is one way to approach the world." You are open and you allow the senses of wilderness and place to enter into you. It goes through you, and that's very good. You hang on to nothing, but in return, there is also not much for you in terms of sustenance and in terms of mirrors that can teach you, because there is very little effort in that kind of wandering. There is an openness, but there is very little discernment.

I'd like you to think about that just for a moment, and think of wandering aimlessly through a desert or a wilderness. Feel not much of a center of gravity. Feel no direction. Feel no real moorings or pulling for you to go one way or another. Take several minutes and let yourself be open to all that happens. What does this feel like?

Take a moment.

Now experience morning, through the day, and into the night, wandering and lost in a wilderness place, but by choice, so you are open and not full of fear. Just experience the feeling of wandering from one trail to the next. You feel no compulsion to be anywhere.

Take several minutes to experience what this is like for you.

(Pause)

Taking a deep breath, let that image fade away. This time I want you to move your consciousness and your imagination into your shaman area around your navel, around your area of intent. I want you to sit down in that same desert wilderness place on a log somewhere, and think to yourself that you trust in the Great Spirit to place his hand at your back, to be there for you, to support you in your movements through life, in your choices.

This time, instead of wandering aimlessly in the desert, start out with an intent. Perhaps it is to find very sacred herbs. Perhaps it is to practice your gate of power, walking silently on the face of Mother Earth. Perhaps you are going to a sacred circle in which you hope to pray or make a rites of passage ceremony. Perhaps you are moving toward a path of enlightenment, and when you come to the fork in the trail, you know which way to go. Perhaps you are just trying to release tension and commune with your god. But with each step that you take, you feel an openness and a perception that allows you to feel the world and all of the existence around you, the beauty of nature. But still, with every step, you know where you're going. You have planned the purpose of your journey, remembering again that this could be a journey where you are searching for a different mirror. Perhaps you meditate in front of a saguaro cactus and experience the shamanlike quality of its existence. Perhaps you sit with the beauty of a flower, and you think about the meaning of beauty and the essence of beauty and how it is a message from the Great Spirit to your own heart.

(Pause)

I'll leave you for several minutes to go walking in beauty within your intent, within your own wilderness, remembering to stay open but also directed within your own heart. Does this feel better than aimless wandering or do you dislike the responsibility that is created by having a direction?

...

(Long Pause)

Presently you smell cedar incense drifting on the air, and you look for its source. Up ahead you see a shrinelike setting under several tall cottonwood trees. You recognize a sacred place of ceremony and a rock altar. You walk closer and marvel at the beautiful prayer sticks, candles, and sacred figures of every kind. At first you feel as if you are intruding. Then, you are startled by a sudden movement. An old native woman with long gray braids walks out of the trees. She welcomes you.

Take a moment to see or sense her clearly.

(Pause)

The old woman asks you why you have come to the sacred world altar of forgetting and remembering. This is an altar of transformation and is appropriate for your rite of passage, whatever it may be. There are no accidents. You have come here for a reason. Speak to this woman now. She is a woman "who knows how." She has great wisdom and will answer the questions in your heart.

Take some time.

Now the old woman shows you a path through the trees. She says, "Wander with intent, my child, and find the four altars of feminine passage ahead of you. At each altar, sit and pray. Find a symbol for that passage, say a prayer, and leave something behind that has held you back. You will hear my voice as you walk. Go now—it is time." She then looks at the sun as it gets lower in the sky.

You begin to walk, feeling different and lighter in some way. You feel blessed. As you round a turn in the trail, an altar of stone is before you on which are carefully placed flowers. You hear the old woman's voice. "This is the altar of puberty and first blood. Sit before it and think of your own passage through puberty. Were your emotions heard and understood? Think a moment and place a stone on the altar, representing an emotion that you felt in adolescence that is somehow holding you back now. After your giveaway, design a symbol for your passage through puberty and remember it. Say a prayer and leave something behind that has held you back emotionally."

Take time.

You leave the altar with respect and you move on down the trail. The wind has come up slightly and you feel it against your skin. The sun is low in the sky, leaving long shadows along the trail before you. As you move around an outcropping of rock you see ahead of you and to the right at the side of a pool of springwater a beautiful altar made out of a slab of stone that has many goddess icons of fertility and union set upon it. There's a carving in stone of two large cotton-wood trees with their trunks intertwined in an infinity symbol. The two cottonwoods represent the balance of the father shield, the branches of the tree reaching up into the sky, bringing that energy down from the universe, from father sky, and down through the branches and the trunk of the tree and back down into the earth, where the roots go deep down into the female shield of Mother Earth. The two trees stand entwined, representing two equal beings standing in perfect union and yet separate—both standing alone and yet in the process of marriage.

You sit before this altar and you think about the passage of marriage and union, or perhaps divorce, if that is the passage that you have also been through, and you close your eyes and say a prayer, feeling the energy and the power emanating from this altar. There is incense burning on the altar—copal. It smells pungent and smokes heavily. The smoke blesses you and touches you lightly. You think of your own passage into union, what that meant to you, and what, perhaps, was a mental idea that you had about that passage, a concept that, perhaps, was not fulfilled, or that was fulfilled beautifully. If you have moved through the gateway of divorce from a state of union or marriage, or if you have not, or if you are looking toward marriage and never have been in a state of union, I would like you to think about something that you need to leave behind on this altar. A leaf from one of the cottonwood trees nearby can represent this. Place the leaf on the altar, and say to the Great Mother, who is the goddess of this altar, that you give away a mental attitude, an idea, that perhaps is old baggage for you, that you no longer need to carry. Then find a symbol for this passage.

I'll give you some time.

Say a prayer of thanks to the altar and bless the altar.

You stand up and move down the trail. You feel, somehow, lighter now, and you realize that the trail is taking you in a circle. Up ahead, not far down the trail, you begin to hear flute music. It calls to you and beckons you to move even more quickly down the trail. It is very beautiful music, and you know that you are looking, now, for the altar of childbirth.

Soon you come upon a cave off to your left, this time in a gathering of rocks. The cave is a natural one. You go to it and you have to bow down to enter through the doorway. Inside the cave you see an altar against one wall. There are candles burning, there are flowers, and there is a Mayan goddess figure of a woman giving birth to a child.

Still, you hear the flute music. You look around for someone. You look out of the cave entrance, and hanging from a branch of a pine tree is a wooden flute. Feathers and ribbons of red satin hang from it. To your amazement you see that the wind is playing through the flute a beautiful melody that touches your heart.

You turn and sit before the altar. You look at this beautiful figure of a woman giving birth, and you think back to your own birthing and perhaps to the time you have given life to children, and you think about what that means to you. Perhaps you have never had a child and did not want to. Think about that decision. Think about what that means to you. If you have had children, perhaps there was an emotion, an idea, that no longer serves you. But most important there was, perhaps, a physical aspect of your life that has held you back on your journey toward enlightenment. Think of that now. What is it physically that has held you back from making a rite of passage, from moving through these gateways toward your completion in the sacred round of spirit?

Take some time now to place a small stone on the altar before the goddess, the Mayan figure, as a giveaway for what you will leave behind on that altar that has held you back physically from taking your power. Also, find a symbol for this passage.

Make your prayers in front of the altar of childbirth and place a flower, from a basket of flowers that has been set in front of the altar, onto the altar with blessings and honor.

You move out of the cave, feeling much lighter and with a tremendous sense of nurturing and caring from the altar that you have just seen.

You walk down the trail toward a grove of aspen and poplar trees by a stream. As you walk along the stream, the path turns to moss. An altar set on a little rise above the fast-moving stream is before you. It is a magnificent altar with a great dreaming bear carved into it and guarding it. She is at once compassionate and ferocious as she looks out at you with her stony gaze.

On this altar many things have accumulated. There are candles and prayer sticks. There are red sashes. There are many pieces of dried moss. Moss represents in some of the Sisterhood's ceremonies, the beginning of puberty and first blood. Sometimes we offer the moss that we took in those ceremonies back onto the altar when we move into the time of wise-blood, when we become changing women going through the gateway that is presided over by Woman at the Edge of Two Worlds.

There are two staffs standing on either side of this altar. I would like you now to tie two ribbons to these very ancient, carved staffs. You look at them closely, running your fingers up and down the carvings on this staff. You see that they represent women in all the stages of their rites of passage throughout their lifetimes. The carvings are beautiful.

You then sit before the altar, and you think about your own passage into the time of wise-blood, the time of holding your blood and holding your power. You think about what it means to go into the second half of your life and how important it is to reach this time, because it is the gateway and the beginning of, truly, your sacred life. But you may have feelings and ideas that you need to give away— perhaps terrors of getting older in a culture where youth is truth. So you pick up two blue ribbons, and you tie one on the left staff, which is what is inside you—the emotions, the ideas that are holding you

back from this gateway. On the right staff you tie a ribbon that is a
promise to yourself for a new attitude, a new way of seeing your life
in the future when you move through the gateway of Woman at the
Edge of Two Worlds. Find a symbol for this passage.

I'll give you some time.

Say a prayer before leaving this altar. Leave something behind that
has held you back.

Having now experienced the difference between wandering aimlessly through the wilderness and wandering through the wilderness
with intent and with ceremony, but still remaining open, I hope you
can see in your own life the difference. If you are a wanderer through
life, afraid to commit, afraid to take responsibility, afraid to create
mirrors so that you can begin to know yourself intimately, you are a
wanderer in space, and the mirrors are very transparent for you. You
don't learn very much from the ones that are created, because they
don't belong to you. They belong to the world itself.

When you were wandering in the desert aimlessly, did that feel like
your life, or do you wish it were?

Take some time.

Take a deep breath and remember what you found so you can
write it in your journal.

One of the great teachings of the sacred gourd is the void, the
openness that is created within the heart of the gourd. If you hold
your gourd up in your mind's eye and turn it in your hands, there is a
hollowness that is felt. You become aware of a kind of tone that hap-

pens when you touch the gourd with the ends of your fingers. There is a timpani there—you could create a drum of a kind. There is an openness and a possibility. When you are open, you are full of possibility. The mystery of life has a chance to enter you and create its power within you and with you. If you are not open, the Great Spirit himself could tap you on your shoulder and you would not be aware of it.

So one of the great teachings of the gourd is to understand openness, the mystery that is contained within nothingness—no thought, no direction, and yet filled with the quality of will and intent. Perhaps that sounds contradictory, and in a sense it is, but what we are creating as shamans together, young travelers in this world of mystery, is a point of view. One of the most important teachings we learn from the gourd is how to form a point of view so that when you move out into the world, you move out from a platform of power and strength and integrity because you do have a sense of your own truth.

Take a deep breath and slowly come back into the room, remembering to write down your impressions.

What are four good things that you keep out of your personal experience, out of your heart, when your heart is closed?

How do you feel wandering aimlessly through the wilderness, open and without fear?

Did journeying with intent feel better than aimless wandering, or did you dislike the responsibility that is created by having a direction?

What did you leave behind at each altar? At the altar of puberty, what did you leave that has kept you back emotionally? At the altar of union, what mental attitude did you give away? What did you leave on the altar of childbirth that has held you back physically from taking your power? What ideas and emotions did you leave behind on the altar of wise-blood?

Think about your passage into the time of wise-blood. You have made a promise to yourself for a new way of seeing your life in the future. Describe your new attitude as you move through the gateway of Woman at the Edge of Two Worlds.

LASHIKA

JOURNEY OF THE FEMALE SPIRIT

✧ ✧ ✧ ✧ ✧ ✧ ✧ ✧ ✧ ✧ ✧ ✧ ✧ ✧ ✧

Introduction

I want you to imagine that you are taking part in an ancient ceremony somewhere in the far north. But first read my description of Lashika, the she-wolf, as she experiences different aspects of her own femaleness and wildness, perhaps very similar to your own hidden qualities. Then begin to see yourself in this same faraway forest. You, too, will be witnessing a feminine rite of passage from a secret place beneath the trees. Lashika and you will both be fascinated by the ceremony before you.

Ceremony/Meditation

Take a deep breath, and move into the center of the words that I speak.

...

Lashika, the she-wolf, her eyes glittering like amber flames in the darkness, was curled up around her pups. They slept in a dark cave dug out of the side of a mountain by slow-moving glaciers centuries ago. Her belly was full and normally she would sleep through the long night and day following, but carried on the high north wind was an unfamiliar sound. She raised her head, suddenly alert, listening for danger, anything that would harm the life of her small family. She was the female alpha wolf, strongest, black, most powerful of her kind. The rest of her pack and her mate were sleeping, curled and quiet in their dream, but Lashika sensed something exciting in the air, something that stirred her heart and the life force of the Great Spirit that ran through every cell in her body.

Slowly, trying not to disturb her pups, she crept to the entrance of the cave. She looked up at the night sky. The waning moon was at its zenith. She sniffed the air and tasted the scent of cedar smoke. She listened. Now she was fully awake. There was singing. Every once in a while, the high north wind would bring the sounds to her of she-human voices, and then the wind would shift. She could sense a drumbeat far in the distance. Her curiosity got the best of her. She looked around in all of the four directions. Not a leaf was stirring. Occasionally, a west wind would move along the ground and ruffle the thick fur that was growing black and tinged with white around her neck, preparing her for the long winter months ahead. Stealthily, she reached out with her paws and stretched. Then she moved down the trail leading into an aspen forest where the music seemed to be coming from. She moved in silence at a strong gallop down a deer trail leading directly into the center of the trees. The sound of the music, drums beating, the voices of women high in song, came closer and closer as she galloped through the night under the protection of the towering trees. It was late fall and unusually warm. She was excited and happy to be moving down a trail in darkness, her favorite time to hunt, to move into the unknown.

Soon the singing became quite loud and the earth pulsated with the beat of a great life drum. She moved off the deer track and into the underbrush, squatting down, moving still quickly and stealthily through the underbrush, her belly touching the ground as she moved, hardly creating a sound. She was fascinated. Her ears pricked forward, listening to every sound that came her way. She could smell the pungent scent of cedar smoke. There was a light at the center of the forest, glowing like a giant sun in a midnight sky. Now she crept along underneath the brush and chokecherry bushes, the pads of her paws feeling the damp leaves beneath them, cushioning any sound that she could have made.

She pulled herself to the edge of a low ridge and looked down into the sacred circle of the Sisterhood of the Shields. She had known these women throughout her life. They had brought her great power in their ceremonies, and she had given them some. They had seen her occasionally on the edge of a canyon or standing atop a hill in the distance. Never had they been this close to one another, but they had honored each other in their respective rituals, each gaining respect and knowledge from the other's existence. Lashika spread her paws in front of her. She stretched her toes and gripped the earth with her claws. Enjoying the ceremony before her, she rested her head down on her paws but was ready to spring into flight if necessary. She understood that something sacred was happening and that she was in no real danger.

A woman wearing a white doeskin beaded dress with fringe, a red sash, and beautiful red beaded moccasins stood in the center of the circle. She was offering sacred ties, tiny medicine bundles that represented different aspects of her life. She was giving these away to a sacred circle made out of stone before her. Within that circle were prayer sticks, four shields, and baskets. Lashika could not see the contents of the baskets; some appeared to be filled with food, human food of some kind. She sniffed the air. It was pungent with cedar smoke and sweet grass. There were many women gathered. These women were elders. They were grandmothers. Occasionally, the fire would spit into the air, sending sparks in a spiraling action on a gust of wind. Then the faces of the women would be illuminated, their ancient brown skin tanned from the sun, the lines of time and life experience etched into their faces. Lashika was curious about their eyes. She always looked into the eyes of the beings that she met, and she read their age, their abilities, their power, their fear. She saw not fear in these eyes but a power that she had not seen in other human faces that she had encountered in her life. She understood their vision. It was almost as if they could speak the same language. It was the language of the wilderness, the understanding of the primordial balance of nature and survival of the fittest in a world of untamed beauty. She sighed deeply, not fully understanding the depth of her perception.

The women did a slow dance in a circle for a long time. The one woman dressed in white in the center continued to pray at the altar in the sacred circle. She must be the alpha human, Lashika thought to herself. She sniffed the air again in recognition of another powerful female in her midst. If she were to move into a position of combat, protection of her young, this would be the human she would have to fight. She knew inside herself that she would win. Lashika was born to be the leader of the pack and never once in her life had she wavered from the understanding of her own power. As she looked at this woman performing a ritual in front of her with her prayer sticks and the dancing fire and the song of the women's voices and the drumming coming somewhere from the shadows around the circle, she honored her. She felt compassion, if that were possible, similar to what she felt for her pups. There was a heartfelt connection to this woman. Slowly, the woman turned from her ceremony and looked toward Lashika. She searched the darkness, feeling the predatory eyes of the she-wolf, which was her medicine, her power animal in the spirit world. She felt the support and the acknowledgment; if not in the physical world, she felt it in spirit.

She turned again as two women raised an elk skin above their heads. The women had long gray braids that reached to their waists. They were dressed in beautiful bright colors from another land, red and pink embroidered *huipiles* and yellow and blue long woven skirts. The tiny threads shone like a parade of fireflies in the yellow light. They were women from nations south of the continent on which they stood. The woman in white doeskin bent low, dancing to the rhythms, and walked beneath the elk skin. She was crying now. She forgot the sense of the wolf and her presence. She forgot everything that was around her, and she grieved for the passing of life as she had known it. She grieved for the passing of her fertility, her ability to have children. She cried and wailed to the waning moon and knew, as Lashika sensed, that her life was changed forever. This was not a tragic passing or a passing of dishonor, but a passage into a new world on the other side of the elk skin. She was now a woman of wise-blood. The women gathered around her, dancing with a wild abandon. They threw something from their fingers that created sparks in the air, and they laughed and they cried and they held one another in the celebration of their birth into the new goddess life.

Lashika lifted her head and cocked it to one side. She recognized the energy coming from these women. It was not unlike the energy coming from her own wolf pack when they honored Lashika as the leader. Like these women, she was the one who went down the paths of life and returned to give the others strength and knowledge and wisdom. She was honored. She understood this woman somehow. She respected her from the depth of her being, and she lent her spirit to their dance.

At this moment Lashika becomes also aware of you. She looks across the ceremony and into the forest. Only a huntress like an alpha wolf could detect your well-hidden presence. Because of the sacredness of the night and the presence of such love among all these powerful women, you and Lashika respect each other's presence without fear. You look into each other's eyes and honor each other's femaleness.

As you both continue to watch the ceremony from the shadows of the forest, you feel like you have gone back a thousand years in time to a ceremony not unlike what your ancestors might have performed long ago. You see a young girl move out of the circle of older women. She is being led by a grandmother and someone who seems to be her mother's age. They dance together, facing the fire and then facing the moon. You sense the love between the young girl and her mother, whose long black hair is knotted at the nape of her neck and tied with bright red ribbons to match her dress. You sense the feeling of honor and respect between the elder woman with long, gray braids to her waist, wearing a doeskin dress with fringe at her ankles, and the young girl wearing a white doeskin dress with a red sash symbolizing first blood.

They approach the ceremonial fire. The young girl hands a folded red blanket and tobacco in braids to the older woman. She is honoring her as her teacher. She is saying to the older woman, "Teach me, for I have much to learn." Then she turns to her own mother, and her mother places a garland of flowers around her neck, intermittently spaced with sage and cedar. Then the elder woman and the mother take abalone shells filled with smoking incense and sweet grass, and they bless the young girl. They smudge her, carrying the smoke over her body. The smoke finally meanders into the billowing smoke coming from the dancing flames of the fire.

Then the young girl kneels before the fire, and throwing something into the flames that sparks, she says a prayer to the sacred fire, to the Great Spirit, and to the grandparents, asking for guidance on her journey. She understands that a new life is upon her, that it is a very important passage, first blood, that she is moving now into a different season of her life. Her moons have begun. Her power has begun. Her receptivity to the seed of life is being felt within her womb, and she knows that marriage and union come next and fertility and the creation of life. She looks forward with joy and excitement to what is ahead of her. She's not afraid of the unknown. She welcomes the unknown with excitement and a sense of respect. She opens her heart to what is new and to her destiny. She then blesses the fire, the grandmother, and her mother, and then the grandmother and the mother stand back from the young girl, honoring her ability to stand alone. The young girl walks around the fire, honoring the four directions, and moves to the opposite side of the circle of women in the ceremony. The grandmother and the mother move to the other side, symbolizing the beginning of adulthood, the beginning of puberty for the young girl. At that point everyone sings and chants and moves in circles around the fire, playing their drums until they come to a place of stillness once again.

Take a moment and think about your own passage into puberty. Did you feel honored?

Take some time.

Out of the ceremonial circle comes another woman, wearing her hair long and not yet in braids, which symbolizes marriage. She is wearing a traditional wedding dress of the Sisterhood of the Shields and beaded moccasins. She is led by a grandmother to the ceremonial fire, and there is great rejoicing in the chant that the women sing, as the young girl is honored with a crown of sweet grass and flowers. She is being honored in a way that is sacred to the Sisterhood of the Shields. In traditional Native American medicine, these ceremonies are different among different tribes and different nations. This is a ceremony for the Sisterhood of the Shields. They honor this young woman, filing past her in a snakelike dance through the smoke from the fire that is now drifting down closer to the earth because of the clouds that have come in with the fog settling over the forest. The moon shines through the clouds, lining them with silver and gold, which gives an awesome translucent, almost iridescent, quality to the setting. The clouds, like a gossamer veil, shroud the fire and the ceremonial women for moments and then lift high on the gentle wind that blows. For a moment you see the wolf's eyes glint amber gold in a flare of firelight.

Finally, the young girl in her wedding dress dances a circle representing the circle of life, and she remembers, with gourd seeds laid near the altar of the sacred fire, her past and her rites of passage with puberty. She offers prayers to the sacred fire as the grandmother takes corn and symbols of fertility and places them in a marriage basket, symbolizing the marriage of the physical world to spirit, and the world of higher consciousness to the apprentice. The young girl, after circling the fire and honoring the four directions, returns to the outer circle. Again the women chant, and again their voices raise high in song with respect and honor in this time of passage.

Take a moment to think about your own feelings about marriage. Have you prepared for union, or if you are married, was it a sacred passage?

Take some time.

Then a woman steps out from the ceremonial circle, obviously pregnant, to celebrate and honor the birthing rites of passage. She circles the fire with an elder woman, with honor and rejoicing in her heart. She kneels before the fire and offers a prayer, a prayer of thanksgiving, and a prayer for the life that is quickening in her womb. The elder woman places her hand on the younger woman's belly, and together they pray for new life and an honoring of destiny. Then the elder woman presents her with a beautiful white flower. She pins it in her hair for the honoring of the flowering of womanhood. Together they circle the fire, honoring the power of the four directions and the wisdom of the Great Spirit, who is about to bring forth life. The woman, honoring her elder woman and teacher, returns to the ceremonial circle. They dance for a long time, symbolizing the passage of time between one rite of passage and another during a woman's life. Many things are represented in this dance. Women wear masks for different passages that they have needed to understand more fully, even if they are elder women. Perhaps during the course of their lives they did not have the opportunity to celebrate the rites of passage in this way.

Take a moment to think about your feelings about having a child or if your pregnancy was celebrated.

Now from out of the circle comes a woman. She is another woman in menopause and she again wears a white, long doeskin dress with a red sash, but this time it is tied differently from the red sash of puberty. It represents the holding of wise-blood, the holding of power. She is a woman in the process of menopause, the most important gateway, ceremony, of the Sisterhood of the Shields, because it marks the beginning of your sacred time as a woman. All other passages are preparation, in a sense, for the gateway of menopause, and in this ceremony she is preparing to meet with Woman at the Edge of Two Worlds. She has been preparing for a long time for this meeting, and you, watching from the forest, see the intensity on her face. You see the joy at this passage and also the tears for what is left behind. They are tears of joy and they are tears, perhaps, for some fear of the unknown. This woman has had her children, she has enjoyed many rites of passage, and now her fertility is over. She gladly moves into the gateway, welcoming with great expectation in her heart the meeting with Woman at the Edge of Two Worlds, the goddess who initiates the women of wise-blood. She looks forward to riding the great horse that represents what we call the hot flash, when your body purifies and balances and rebalances the hormonal structure of your body so that higher consciousness has a place to live within your being.

The woman approaches the fire with her two elder teachers. She bows down to the fire, bending at her waist and begins to dance, and she sings from her heart and from her soul. She sings a song of power. She calls for her power animal to join her as she makes this transit into her sacred time. All the women play their drums, honoring this great moment for their sister. The women who have moved to the ceremonial fire before her come now to the sacred fire, and they give a gift to this woman in hopes that she will remember them in her prayers and in hopes that her journey will be a fine and a sacred one. They dance together, young girl, pregnant woman, woman of union and marriage, and woman of menopause. Finally, they stand in the four directions around the fire, and they pray to the four directions, to the Great Spirit, to the sacred fire, and to the guardians of the gateways of knowledge and wisdom.

Then four women, carrying an elk hide, approach the fire, and the woman of menopause walks under the elk skin, covered by a veil, symbolic of the sleep that so many of us live through in our earlier lives, the sleep of our consciousness that is so unaware of not only our own needs but also of the needs of our great Mother Earth, the needs of our spirit. The veil represents how we deny our spirit expression in our physical life. It represents our ignorance. The lifting of the veil as the woman reaches the other side of the elk skin symbolizes the lifting of ignorance, the tearing away of the veil of illusion so that she can balance herself. Walking out into life, manifesting her dreams with a foot in the physical and a foot in spirit. She is balanced, so her expression and her wisdom become complete. Her sacred life and her true sisterhood begin.

As you sit watching these ceremonies from the forest, fascinated by the play of shadows and leaping flames, the strangeness and yet the deep love and honoring of another culture celebrating their sacred rites of passage, you feel, perhaps, a longing within yourself to create a rites of passage for yourself. You realize how you possibly have not honored within yourself the passages that you have attained. You may have passed over them, not acknowledging their power and importance in your life, and therefore, perhaps you lessened your own chances to grow and to manifest your dreams. For a moment you feel your energy rise. You feel within yourself a need to step forward and become a full participant in this fire ceremony yourself. Perhaps you see yourself creating your own ceremony with other women, other sisters, going through their passages, honoring them, helping them to grow and become all that they can become. Perhaps you see yourself interacting with me or with Agnes Whistling Elk or a teacher like us. Perhaps you see yourself walking out of the forest and going down to the fire, giving a gift to an old wise woman who is dancing there, who is perhaps waiting for you.

You feel your energy bringing you toward that special time, a time when that fire will be for you. It is possible that next time the Sisterhood meets, it will be your time. The fire will be for your celebration and your initiation.

Take a moment and think about what that means to you. Perhaps you've never thought about celebration or initiation or rites of passage as something that meant anything special, or when you went into puberty, you hoped nobody noticed. So many of us have felt that way. We hope nobody notices the beginning of blood. How do you feel about that? How do you feel, really, about menopause? Do you want the men in your life to know about menopause, or are you trying to hide these sacred passages from view? Do you want to appear younger? Do you not want to appear strange in any way?

·Take a moment to think about this.

Take some time.

Now I want you to see yourself still in the forest, watching the cer-emony, and suddenly the dancing and the music stop. Agnes Whistling Elk, a beautiful elder woman with long, gray braids to her waist, wearing a beaded doeskin dress and beaded moccasins, turns her piercing eyes toward where you hide in the forest. You realize that she has known that you were there all along. She holds up her arms, and she asks you to join her, and come to the center of the fire. You're frightened and yet full of excitement, because you really wanted to dance all along to the rhythm of the drums. You come down out of the underbrush, proud, because you're proud of being a woman, and you're proud of what you have become. You join the circle. You come and you walk toward the sacred fire. Agnes holds out her arms to you with a wonderful smile and a hint of humor in her eyes, and she puts her arms around you and holds you very close for a moment. She feels your heart against her own. And then she steps back and holds your face in her hands. She looks at you in the eyes, not to make you feel uncomfortable, but to communicate with you on the deepest level. She asks you a question.

I'll give you a moment to find this question.

Then she asks you what it is that you need from her. What is it that you wish her to tell you, to give you, or to teach you?

I'll give you a moment.

Agnes is happy with her conversation with you, and she says that all people who approach the sacred fire must give away to the sacred fire and make a prayer to the fire and to the Great Spirit and to the Great Mother who teaches us and gives us life. She gives you first a gift for you to keep and then asks you to give away something to the fire. It could be a strand of your own hair or it could be something that you wish to throw into the fire. It could be a crystal, a stone, a piece of paper with something written on it.

I'll give you time to do that now.

Now that your prayers have been made, Agnes hands you a drum. It's beautiful and feels like slick leather under your fingers, very ancient. The picture of a blue star is on the face of the drum and a whistling elk is painted on the other face of the drum. She gives you a mallet and says, "Do as I do. Follow me." And you follow her in a simple step, swaying this way and that to the music, to the drumming, to the rhythms created by these magnificent women. You look at their faces as she takes you around the circle and gives you the opportunity to look into the eyes of all of the women of the Sisterhood of the Shields and also the women who have celebrated their passage this night. You get a new sense of what it means to be a powerful, beautiful elder woman.

I'll give you several minutes as you walk around the circle, looking into the eyes of wisdom, at the women of the Sisterhood of the Shields, representing their people, their sacredness, from all over the world. They are forty-four in number.

As you walk around the circle of women, you realize that there is a shift in the expression in their eyes. They become less remote. In fact, the women seem to be closing the circle around you. Then, Agnes Whistling Elk speaks to you.

"We accept you as a woman who is seeking to define her own truth in the world. We honor your presence among us. We honor your individuality. We honor your unique feminine creativity, and we crown you with a halo of divine light. You are made of light, because light is love. Open your heart to the rites of passage that beckons to you.

"As you walk across this new plateau of celebration, take a moment to sit within the silence of your own being and envision the rites-of-passage altar that belongs to you. Smell the beautiful flowers placed on it, the cedar incense burning, and hear the tiny bells ringing in the gentle wind."

Take a deep breath and go deeply into that place of silence and serenity within you. As you honor your altar, you will see or sense the guardians of that altar appearing to you. Everyone sees the guardians differently, because eveyone's energies are different. You may see angels, a power animal, a goddess figure, or an old wise one. For those at the gateway of menopause, the guardian goddess is Woman at the Edge of Two Worlds. Let these beings manifest to you in all of their glory. They will have a message for you about your coming initiation, so listen well to their words. If you do not visualize well, simply sense the presence of a goddess figure near you. They are everywhere around you.

I will give you some time.

Now that you have honored your altar and your guardian spirits, you realize as you gaze into the central fire that this fire is for you as well, and will burn like a sacred light within your heart during your coming initiation. You honor this blessed circle of women as they give you hugs and flowers.

•••

Then, as images of the sacred circle begin to fade, you look toward the forest where you last saw Lashika, the wolf. The ceremony would not be complete without seeing her one last time. You look toward Lashika, and she looks for one piercing moment into your eyes.

Lashika has been watching the ceremony with fascination, but she knows it is time to return to her wolf den and her pups. Lashika could feel a stirring in her belly; she knew that they were missing her. Very quietly she honored the circle that she had witnessed. She lifted her head to the sky, took a long, deep breath of the sacred smoke, and then she turned and stealthily moved through the undergrowth. The moon was now very low in the sky, and an eerie light was on the horizon. It was the hour of the wolf, the time that Lashika knew best. She crept away from the ceremony, her feet touching the earth lightly with each beat of the drum. She raised up into a gallop, her powerful haunches striding through the darkness, leading her home. Her heart was full for her sister-beings. She had witnessed the birth of a new kind of existence and life force. It was the birth of a teacher into the world of wisdom. It was the birth of sister-beings in spirit, who, not unlike herself, moved with courage into the world, gathering the knowledge that they found every day, bringing it home to their brothers and sisters so that they might live in harmony and sacred balance on Mother Earth.

Lashika paused at the top of a hill. Throwing her great head back, she closed her eyes to the shine of the moon and uttered a cry from the depths of her spirit. Her wolf song was for the beauty in life and called out for a sisterhood between all female beings. Lashika's voice echoed through the mountains long after she was gone.

•••

Slowly take a deep breath and let the images completely fade away. Come back into the room, taking another deep breath. If you have your journal with you, before you speak to anyone, write down what you found in the meditation.

✦ ✦ ✦ ✦ ✦ WORKSHEET ✦ ✦ ✦ ✦ ✦

Think about your own passage into puberty. Did you feel honored? Explore your feelings about marriage, about union. Have you prepared for union? If married, was it a sacred passage? What are your feelings about having a child? Was your pregnancy celebrated?

How do you feel about menopause? Do you want the men in your life to know about menopause, or are you trying to hide these sacred passages from view. Do you want to appear younger? Do you not want to appear strange in any way? Are your feelings similar to the feelings you had with first blood?

Are you proud of what you have become as a woman? What is it that you are proud of?

What is your question for Agnes Whistling Elk? What is it that you wish her to tell you or teach you?

Write down your prayer that you gave away to the sacred fire.

SEED POD

THE CIRCLE OF LIFE

❖ ❖ ❖ ❖ ❖ ❖ ❖ ❖ ❖ ❖ ❖ ❖ ❖ ❖ ❖ ❖

Ceremony/Meditation

Close your eyes, please, and take a deep breath.

Have you ever thought about the beginning of existence? Have you ever thought about the creation of life, the beginnings of all life? As it has been taught to me by my teachers, in the beginning was a great mystery. The mystery was the sacred void, the nothingness of pure bliss. Out of this nothingness came an overflowing of love, and from that love was created the life force that became animated in many places around the universe. That animation is the life that we see today on our great Mother Earth. That animation was created from movement. Out of the seed pod of genetics and chemical order was created movement between the polarities of positive and negative energy. The positive and negative energies were given names. The negative became female; the positive became male. And there was an attraction and a repulsion that pulled the energies together and drew them apart. Out of that polarity was created the sacred dance of life, the sacred spiral of movement and existence. In the legends throughout history, these positive and negative poles of energy were given form and names by different peoples. They became legends of creation, creation myths. And out of those creation myths came a philosophy and a religion and a way of life.

At the core of all creation myths is movement, and deeper into the process of movement is the silent darkness of bliss and nothingness from which all comes and to which all returns. We are made from stars and to the stars we must return one day. You have heard me say this over and over again, and that is because the knowledge has its source somewhere in the night sky, we are told from the Pleiades. In a sense we are all star pods on this earth with a destiny to become enlightened, to create mirrors in our lifetime through the process of movement and life force, mirrors that enhance our fulfillment and the evolvement of our spirit. We have an ancient longing to return home, home to the source of all that is.

The Great Spirit asks you to celebrate your birth. Celebrate this great opportunity that is your life, this wonder that contains the mysteries of all that has ever lived. You are all that has ever lived. You know everything, if only you could access the ancient memory contained within your subconscious mind in a celebration to the Great Spirit.

I would like you now to curl up on the floor in an embryonic form, as if in fact you are a great, mysterious seed pod containing the origins and mysteries of life. Use your imagination. Fold your body tightly together like a bud in readiness to be born and matured.

Take a moment.

Now, as you are curled up on the floor, think of yourself as a never-ending circle. Touch as many parts of your body to other parts of your body, so that there is a circle of current, round and round and round. When you are a seed pod, you are contained and you hibernate, perhaps through many long winters to another season, when you are planted, when there is water, when there is sunshine, and you burst forth into a new and different life, a form of life that reaches up to the sun.

See yourself now in the hibernating period. Perhaps you are beneath the earth. Perhaps you are in a seed pod, waiting to be planted. Think for a moment about the wonders that you contain, what is within you, what a miracle it is that you contain the possibilities of life and the remembrance of who you are. As a seed pod, you can never be other than what you are. If you are a seed pod that contains a giant pine tree, you could never be other than a pine tree. Think for a moment: we as human beings can be so many things. We cannot be a horse, and we cannot be a daisy, but as human beings we can express ourselves as a daisy or as a horse. We can become a scientist or a writer. We can become anything we want to be. As a seed pod, there is a destiny that is written by the gods long before you were formed. So remember that destiny of beauty and perfection as you lay dormant now through the long winter. Imagine yourself as having been planted somewhere in the earth. Feel the nurturing energy of Mother Earth holding you.

Take a moment.

(Pause)

···

Then, gently you begin to see and feel and sense that there is some light and there is moisture, spring rains. You can smell the rains, smell the moisture on the grasses, on the trunks of the trees, on the leaves. And slowly, ever so slowly, you begin to open. As you open, you uncurl your arms, your branches, your legs, the trunk of this extraordinary tree. Slowly, slowly—take plenty of time. You begin to open as if you are a flower becoming receptive, magnificently female, open to Father Sun, coming down with a smile from the sky to make you whole, to help you to live, to help you to express your perfection into the world. You open with your arms wide, and you lift up toward the sun. You kneel; then you stand, perhaps to get even closer to the nourishment of the heat. And then in the process of flowering, you begin to move, turning gently to face the sun.

(Pause)

You move, catching pollen on your petals, on your branches, catching the wind, the drops of rain, and you become fragrant with spring and the process of living.

Take several minutes as you begin to grow and become whole. Let time elapse, and imagine spring turning into summer.

(Pause)

See yourself now as full grown, as a flower, as a bush, as a giant tree. Begin to sway now in the gentle summer wind, and as you sway, you begin to realize that now you too are creating seed pods that will soon loosen from your mother structure and float off on the wind to

begin to become dormant once again. So sway now in the wind.
Sense deep within your biology how things go full circle.

(Pause)

You are flowering now. You are in your prime. Celebrate. Celebrate the magnificence of your body. Dance, now, in celebration for the mystery and the gift of life.

Take some time.

Now that you have rejoiced in your completeness, feel yourself getting older. It is autumn. The summer breezes have left and gone south. It is getting colder, and now when the wind comes there's an icy edge to it. You know that winter is coming. You are on the brink of winter, and you are losing your bloom. Your color is fading, and soon your leaves will be dropping or your petals will be dropping, nourishing Mother Earth, fertilizing, going back into the soil for the spring crop of the following year.

As you dance now, you are a little more stiff. You are older now. You are wiser. There's a wisdom in your movement, and you express it with your arms and your legs and the trunk of your body. You express this newfound knowledge. You have lived. You are superior to those who come after you. You are superior, and yet you are more humble, because you know what life is about.

Feel yourself become older now, and your leaves begin to fall, and as your leaves fall, I'd like you now to become one of the pods that drop from your branches and slowly move down toward the earth. You curl back down onto the floor. You curl and curl around, moving ever so slowly until a complete circle is formed.

Now it is truly winter. Feel yourself being rolled across the earth by the wind. And now there is the first snowfall. You are a bit under-ground. Leaves are comfortably over you, and they keep you warm. You close your eyes and you are sleepy now. You go back into that ancient slumber, the slumber of hibernation and the deep and sacred dream that will lead to transformation, death, and rebirth, all over again. You go to sleep, gently, feeling the breath of Mother Earth and the winds of the Great Mother circling around you, keeping you safe, keeping you whole and protected for the next season of life.

Take several minutes, and then slowly, as it feels comfortable, open your eyes and come back into the room.

✦ ✦ ✦ ✦ ✦ **WORKSHEET** ✦ ✦ ✦ ✦ ✦

What do you think happens at death?

What did you feel about the passage of time as a seed pod?

Did you have a sense of your own cycles in life? Of the seasons and the changes within yourself?

HOPE

SEEING AGING DIFFERENTLY: AGING AS A PROCESS OF BECOMING WORTHY OF WISDOM

VISION

There are times when you will have less vision, and because of that dimness you will become unbalanced in your seeing; you will see everything—every stone, every machine, every tree—as dead rather than alive. As your vision grows, sit still within the city, and begin to develop and to see that stones and plants and even machines are alive. Even the dead trees have passed through the gateway in the west. Their spirit carries the Dreaming Shield. Begin to see the life within every object. Begin to see the sacredness in things, their energy, their colors, their luminous forms—their shadow beings. Then you will become strong. See power all around you; it is you. You have developed true vision.

—The Power Deck

SACRED GOURD WOMAN

FINDING YOUR TRUTH

❖ ❖ ❖ ❖ ❖ ❖ ❖ ❖ ❖ ❖ ❖ ❖ ❖ ❖ ❖ ❖

Introduction

The "sacred gourd" is an ancient teaching done in different ways by many people. In my book *Shakkai, Woman of the Sacred Garden* I wrote about the sacred *hu* and how to find the garden of your own spirit and peace and tranquility that is within the gourd. Sometimes it is better to celebrate the small instead of always bigger and better and more. In *Shakkai* I was taught by my teacher to become as small as a thumb so that I could go into the sacred gourd and find the seeds of wisdom that are planted there, to find an entire universe of power and exploration and discovery.

In my teaching, I've talked a lot about how we have imploded energy throughout the last several decades, always going inside, within, to find the answers that are found within the self-wound. There is an old legend, an old myth, that describes very well this shamanic process. It has to do with the difficulties that we find in our lives, problems that we find and how we deal with our deepest feelings, like grief and unworthiness.

Ceremony/Meditation

Take a deep breath. Relax your entire body. Let go of your worries, your thoughts, your problems, and let your muscles completely relax. Go as deeply as you know how to go. Take another deep breath. Remember that you are in a very protected place, a very sacred place. No harm can come to you, so relax into the arms of the Great Mother and let her comfort you. Forget about your body and allow yourself to hear my words. These words are woven like a tapestry with sacred sounds to open your heart, to help you to feel the power and the sacredness of ideas, oftentimes new ideas. Set your doubt aside and just for a moment let us go together into the world of the sacred dreamtime.

The legend is about a young native woman who is in great emotional pain. She has lost a child. The child has died in an accident, and she does not want to go on living, so she goes out into the wilderness, or symbolically, the unknown territory of her psyche. Her emotional pain is so great that she wants to inflict physical pain upon herself because of her woman's misplaced guilt. She goes for days and days without food and is about to die, and she hopes that she will die. But she wants, as tradition has it, to find a cave, or a place within herself of woman spirit, in which she can lay down and finally at last join the Great Spirit. But the Great Spirit wants to teach her something before she goes on to the spirit world, because she is not yet finished on this earth. She has not yet learned the lesson of grief.

As she walks, barely able to take another step, she finds a tree of thorns, representing the difficulties and trials of life, and she breaks off a branch, wanting to beat herself with these thorns, feeling that her child's death was somehow her own fault. (So many women feel in this life that it is always their fault. If anyone was to blame, it was them. She didn't do enough, she wasn't good enough, she was not special enough to keep this event from happening. If I had done better, everything would still be all right.) The woman tears away the branch of thorns, wanting to move more deeply into the self-wound, causing her fingers to bleed. But power shows her the way, because she has deepened herself through grief and has demonstrated her perseverance. She sees that behind the bush of thorns is a cave entrance. (Behind the pain, deep in the center, is a different way.) She is very relieved. She takes the branch, and crawling under the tree, she finds her way into this cave. Unknown to her, it is a very sacred cave, and it has been waiting for her.

Inside the cave are jewellike female figures with magnificent lights reflecting from their shining surfaces. It's an apparition of sacred totems on the rock walls and around a central fire. She lays down in the cave to die, and as she looks up at the ceiling of the cave in total wonderment she sees a mirror on the ceiling set into the stone. She sees herself looking back at herself. After a long time of looking in this mirror, with the magnificent, sacred icons surrounding her, she begins to see not only the grief but also the foolishness of what she is about to do. She begins to realize that it is not appropriate for her to take her own life.

Presently, she sits up and reaches for a beautiful icon of a goddess figure. It is the goddess figure of wisdom and prayer. She knows the meaning of this goddess, and presently, she begins to pray. As she prays, new strength comes to her. At first she simply sees a gourd. Then, within her vision she sees her own womb from which her child was born transforming into a sacred gourd. She prays for guidance, for teaching. The gourd transforms in her mind, and it begins to shine with a radiant light. She touches it with her spirit hands. At first it feels rough and still has Mother Earth clinging to its sides. In her teaching dream, the spirit of the gourd, an ancient woman, the keeper of the gourds, shows her how to wash her gourd, clean it of the mold and the dirt. As she cleans the gourd, she holds it up to her higher self, that place of strength and power that is beginning to awaken within her third eye.

She turns the gourd in her hands, feeling it now, clean and beautiful, still holding the vibration of Mother Earth. She feels it and she begins to sense the power within the gourd. She knows that there is a life-form within this gourd struggling to be born. She knows she has to cut open the top of the gourd, as Gourd Woman shows her. She touches the gourd and turns it in her hands and thinks. Then she holds it to her heart, bringing her mind down into her heart so she can perceive the voice of the gourd. And the gourd speaks to her. She sees that within the gourd is a kind of oracle, a teacher, that has been brought up from the center of Mother Earth into the sacred void. She is an elder of the universe and is a beautiful expression of new life. The young woman is healed and begins to see life in a new way.

I would like you to take a few minutes and listen to the voice of this sacred gourd. Then see yourself holding the sacred gourd in the cave as if you have been magically transported there in the young woman's place. Feel the gourd in your heart. Hold the gourd up to your third eye. Feel it and sense that there is also a sacred spirit within this gourd that is your teacher, an oracle, so to speak, so that when you are finished painting your gourd, there will be a mirror within this gourd that will reflect you and will speak to you and teach you whenever you look into it. You may see the face of your power animal. You may see an old wise one. You may see an angel. But for now, feel the gourd and begin to hear a voice, a being, speaking to you very gently. This being speaking to you is Gourd Woman. Take a moment to see her beautiful, ancient face and to take her outstretched hands in welcome as she emerges from the gourd. She is here to help you on your journey. Let Gourd Woman speak to you now, and ask her to teach you one lesson, something that you need to know. It is a teaching about your accomplishments. What accomplishments do you feel proud of? Talk to Gourd Woman about your feelings of worthiness and accomplishment. Then listen to what she has to say.

Take some time.

Remember that you have not opened the gourd yet. You have not cut the top off. You are just looking at the gourd in its totality with all of its mysteries and power held within.

Take some time.

Now that you have heard the voice of your gourd and have met Gourd Woman, take the gourd up again, turning it over and over in your hands. This time, because sacred gourds are not familiar to you as yet, you ask Gourd Woman to help you find the place of entrance into this womb world. What you are looking for is a place to enter the gourd, perhaps a spot of coolness or warmth, but an area will call you. It could be halfway down the gourd or near the top. Do not open the gourd yet. Just find a place where you wish to enter.

I'll give you several minutes.

Now I would like you to feel the heartbeat of the gourd. Sense it. There will be an almost subtle pulsation that you will feel in your fingers. As you look at the outside of the gourd, you will see configurations that will seem to develop magically—the way the skin has grown on the outside of the gourd, the way Mother Earth has left her markings on the skin. You will begin to see images of clouds or animals or energy flows. As you do this just keep turning the gourd in your hands, realizing that this is a great force, a great life force waiting to be opened. Feel the heartbeat if you can. You may only sense the heartbeat, but you will feel it. I'll give you some time.

Always remember that your heartbeat is akin to the heartbeat of Mother Earth. As in our drumming, you are as one with the energy and life force of this great planet.

This sacred gourd may have a name, or it may not. But absolutely this gourd can become the extension of your own sacred void within, your own womb. The sacred void within you is part of the essential power of woman. We carry the void as we always have throughout time. But it is important in the world of alchemy, in the world of power and mystery and sacred truth, to learn how to extend that womb outside of yourself. Within this exterior void you will learn to plant the seeds of wisdom that are very special to you and are germinated by the forces of the universe and Mother Earth in the sacred dance of life. Let me show you how this is done.

I want you to feel the sacred gourd that you have been working on. Then see this gourd rotating and slowly moving into the space of your own womb. If you are a man, you still have a space within you in the same place a woman does, but your space is for different purposes. For a man, it is for an expression of your creativity as you marry that creativity with your communication with the Great Spirit. For a woman it is the same, but she also receives the explosion of the male and implodes that energy into an incredible phenomenon called the birth of movement. All people can learn to create motion and life within the sacred gourd. The Taoists did it, the Chinese and the Japanese have done it, and most native people who I have known have evolved in their higher work a system and a way and a love for the gourd and her mysteries.

I want you now to feel and see that the gourd begins to twirl and is gently merging inside you and becoming a part of your lower abdomen. Feel its beauty and its shiny golden, beautiful light, feel the warmth in that part of your body and the sense of power, of magic and alchemy, where all fear, all trouble, in your life is being transformed into pure light, and let that gourd sit within you. Become comfortable with her.

I'll give you a moment.

Now inside yourself there's a password for a word of power, in essence, which you speak, because sound is such great power in our lives, even though we are often not aware of it. The world and your body are held together with sound.

I want you to think of a word, the first word that pops into your mind. It doesn't matter. It could be any word at all, but it is a word of power, because Gourd Woman is helping you and is giving you energy. Take a deep breath and hear that word in your heart.

I'll give you a moment.

If you did not get a word, just choose a word now, a word that you like that means goodness to you and power. Say this word, now, to yourself, and at the same time image the gourd, whether you are a man or a woman, being birthed through the birth canal. See this womb of creativity being born into the world, and hold it out in front of you and let it lie on top of your stomach like a newborn baby. Caress this gourd with your fingers until you know every inch of her.

Take a moment.

Now envision the gourd being circled by green and golden luminous light, and just sit with her. Go into a deep place of meditation, and say over and over again within your mind or within your heart, I Am, I Am, I Am.

Take a few minutes.

Hold up your gourd. Gourd Woman takes out an obsidian knife, very sharp and very sacred. It belongs to the people of the stars. She blesses her knife. She holds it up to the sky fathers and down to Mother Earth. She thanks her ancestors and all those who love us to help us on our way, on our path of truth. Then she places the blade against the gourd, and she thrusts it into the gourd, and she begins to cut off the top. The gourd feels wonderful about this, because what it means to the gourd is release. The gourd, without its top being taken off, has imploded energy, just like you and I, maybe for a long time. That implosion of energy at a certain point must be reversed and expressed into the world, into a manifestation of your sacred dream, of your act of power. In some way it must explode into the world, because otherwise, you are in a state of stasis. You think you are standing still, but you are always going either forward or backward. The gourd feels the same way. It wants to give of its knowledge and its wisdom and its life force.

You know, now, where that place to be cut should be on the top of the gourd because you found it with Gourd Woman. Gourd Woman cuts open the gourd and lifts, finally, the top off. You see a power in the form of golden, white light coming out of the center of the gourd and surrounding not only itself, but you as well. Then Gourd Woman hands you a digging stick with a crystal in a curve-shaped formation tied to the end of the digging stick, and you begin to clean out the gourd. You take the seeds and you put the seeds on sacred red, natural material like felt or silk, and you clean your gourd carefully. Each time you take a swipe with the digging stick, you say a prayer. You say a prayer for spirit, you say a prayer for substance, you say a prayer for your emotions, and you say a prayer for your process of mind in all of the four directions.

I'll give you several minutes.

Now that you are finished with your prayers, Gourd Woman hands you a mirror, a small mirror, and using her spit, which is a symbol of spirit in the spirit world, you and she both use your fingers to adhere the mirror to the bottom of your gourd. And now the world of the sacred gourd has begun. She has been born. Now it is up to you to give her power and strength and to feed her with the energy of your own spirit.

...

Now you take a deep breath, and another, and with great love and great reverence, you give the gourd back to Gourd Woman, who begins to dance with her, offers her to the four directions and blesses her so that her life is a totality and you may begin your next work within her.

Take a breath, and when you are finished, open your eyes and slowly come back into the room.

✦ ✦ ✦ ✦ ✦ WORKSHEET ✦ ✦ ✦ ✦ ✦

What is your word of power? How does it make you feel?

Describe how you experienced your gourd.

Did you feel the heartbeat of your gourd?

What were your impressions when you cut into your gourd?

HOW TO MAKE YOUR GOURD

OPENING THE WOMB OF CREATIVITY

✧ ✧ ✧ ✧ ✧ ✧ ✧ ✧ ✧ ✧ ✧ ✧ ✧ ✧

OPENING AND PREPARING THE GOURD

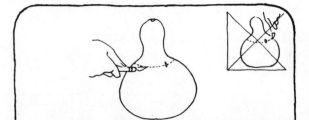

Wash the gourd gently using a soft scrubber to remove loose traces of mold and dirt. Observe the natural patterning. Use your hand to divine the heart of the gourd, then set it flat on a table or on the ground to find the balance point.

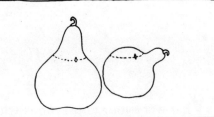

Using a pencil, outline the natural opening, making it large enough to fit your hand, and balanced so the lid won't fall off; mark or notch a line above and below to help realign top with bottom.

Holding gourd securely, make the entry point with a heavy duty cutting blade above the heart of gourd, then very carefully draw the blade back and forth at a right angle to the ground using a sawing motion. (Do not cut straight down, or the lid may fall inside gourd instead of sitting on top.) BE VERY CAREFUL TO CUT <u>AWAY FROM YOU, in case you slip.</u>

Open lid and scoop out seeds and lining; put dust into disposal bag, and save seeds in small plastic bag to make seed bundle for World Altar. Clean inside with sponge or toothbrush then sand the cut edges with sandpaper or fine-grain sandpaper.

Select or mix a color using a paper plate as a palette. Using small sponge square or a brush, paint the inner portion of gourd, both top & bottom. Note the texture and designs inside.

(Optional) While the paint is still wet, sprinkle a little glitter, or glue some crystal chips, gems or pebbles inside the gourd using an epoxy glue.

Paint designs on the outer part of the gourd and let dry. If you wish to create a handle to facilitate removing the top of the gourd, use a shell, wood, crystal, or other object and affix with epoxy glue or drill a small whole and insert a leather thong.

(Optional) To make a headdress, wrap, tie, or glue objects such as crystals, feathers, shells, beads, or twigs in a bundle and affix to gourd. Make sure they are attached securely.

SACRED GARDEN OF YOUR SPIRIT

SERENITY AND PEACE

✦ ✦ ✦ ✦ ✦ ✦ ✦ ✦ ✦ ✦ ✦ ✦ ✦ ✦ ✦ ✦ ✦

Ceremony/Meditation

Take a deep breath and relax your body completely. Take another deep breath, and look up now into the dark heavens. You are looking up into a night sky. See the stars and the Pleiades twinkling in the faraway blackness of space, which is magnificent and huge before you. You see the moon is full, at its zenith, and you look for a long time at the face of the moon.

(Pause)

You see the mottling on the surface of her, and as you look at the irregularities of shadow, darkness, and light, you realize that that is not unlike the mottling quality that Mother Earth has left on the outside of your gourd. In a sense the moon has a great deal to do with your gourd. It is filled with lunar power, and Gourd Woman is a moon goddess and will come to you with great love and illumination for your path of heart.

I would like you now to look at the moon with your spirit eyes. Look intensely into her face, and as you look at the moon, begin to see that a figure is beginning to form. As you watch that figure being born before you and slowly taking human female form, you begin to see that it is the figure of Gourd Woman. She is very old. She is an ancient goddess. She has been around since the beginning of time, since the very beginning of ceremony, since the beginning of the Sisterhood and our work together. She comes to you when higher ceremonies are being made. As you watch her—she will look different for each of you—you sense that she is a very private goddess. Open your heart. She does not wish to be celebrated unless your heart is in the right place. She listens to your heart and the sound of its beat. She listens to your breathing. She listens for your truth.

(Pause)

She moves closer toward you, across the eons of time that appear to separate us all. She comes toward you and into view so that you can begin to see her very clearly.

Take a moment to describe what she is wearing and how she responds to you.

She extends her arm out to you in a gesture of warmth and welcome. You see that she is carrying a gourd. She carries it with her arm around it. The void, or gourd, that she carries is enormous but small enough to carry. She brings it to you and sits down in front of you. She hands the gourd to you, and you open your arms wide to hold it. Both of you sit with your arms around this giant gourd, looking into each other's eyes. She has a lesson of great importance for you. Listen carefully.

I'll give you several minutes.

As you look into the eyes of Gourd Woman, Keeper of the Sacred Gourds, you see her face full of merriment and joy, and yet, a tremendous quality of depth is within her eyes. You see within her a sense of direction, a sense of possibility, a sense of hope. You know that she has an abiding sense of character—she knows who she is—and perhaps you hope to be like her. You look into her eyes and hold with her the void, the sacred void that represents the emptiness and the magic of the universe contained within a single gourd, a magnificent and beautiful creation of earth and spirit that comes from only a single seed planted in Mother Earth. It is for you to contemplate the goodness of your life as you look into her eyes. Open to what life has to give you.

(Pause)

As you hold your gourd, you begin to create a gourd that is yours within your heart. Symbolically, take out of you the knowledge you contain, like you take the seeds out of the gourd, and remember what you have learned, what you have created that is you, and place that intensity into the gourd itself so that you can begin to see tangibly what you have become.

(Pause)

...

This teaching is about celebrating where you are in life, celebrating your accomplishments. I would like you to take several minutes now, and as you still are holding the gourd with Gourd Woman, I would like you to tell her what you have accomplished in your life that you are proud of, and no accomplishment is too small. Take several minutes and share with her what you have created in your life, how you have survived. And you have, indeed, survived a very hard time.

Nobody who has lived through this time in history can say that this time is easy. You have done a lot. No accomplishment is too small. Tell Gourd Woman proudly who you are.

I'll give you several minutes.

In our work we always honor our teachers, where we have come from, and our elders. Every person has two very important people in their life—that person's mother and father. I would like you to think about what was the greatest gift that your mother gave you. What did you learn most from your mother, even if the relationship you had with her was very difficult, even if it was very joyous? Take a moment and tell Gourd Woman about the gift that you learned from your mother.

Take several minutes.

Now that you have remembered the gift of your mother, I want you to think about your father. Tell Gourd Woman what gift your father gave you. What did you learn most from your father?

It's important in this work that you think of the totality of your being from all aspects and the teachings from all directions.

Take a moment.

Now looking into the eyes of Gourd Woman, what is it that you want to learn from this sacred gourd? This gourd is a mirror for you, particularly in this meditation. It is a mirror for your openness or your lack of it, for your ability to direct yourself or your inability to commit to a direction. Openness, if it is to be vital in your life, also asks for commitment from you. Ask for a commitment for openness, for the ability to receive the gifts of life. Allow yourself to be sensitive; allow yourself to discern whether you want to let this person or that person into your heart or into your spirit influence. Don't be so afraid to open your heart. Bring your consciousness into your heart. Slowly feel your heart open. Feel it. Sense it. Slowly, slowly allow the light of the sun to come into the darkest corners of your heart. It's all right if once in a while somebody wanders in that shouldn't be there; simply ask that person to leave. You have the power over your life to discern what your life should be and can be. Sacred gourds will teach you that.

Take a moment and feel this, allowing your heart to stay open. Visualize yourself strong and yet flexible, like a great ponderosa pine, rooted into the earth and yet bending gracefully in the wind.

(Pause)

And now, with Gourd Woman still sitting with you and holding the gourd, I would like you to see yourself getting much, much smaller, very tiny, in fact. But the gourd remains large.

(Pause)

Gourd Woman then places pine ladders up the side of the gourd and down into the gourd. I would like you to see yourself climbing first up and then down the ladder, as if you were going deep into the earth, into a kiva, a sacred space, a place of prayer and ceremony. After climbing up, you step carefully down the ladder with this great teacher-woman ahead of you.

When you reach the bottom of the gourd, you realize the inside of the gourd is a *shakkai,* or "captured landscape," a beautiful garden, a garden that represents the garden of your own spirit. There are trees and flowers that you love in life—roses that you love to smell and lakes that you like to sit next to and see the reflections of the sky and the stars and the moon.

You also sense that there is work to be done here to make this garden yours. Sit in the bottom of your gourd with Gourd Woman and begin to fashion a garden of great beauty and peacefulness and serenity, but a garden that has, again, discernment and art, that is carefully laid out and planned.

Take several minutes to do a very good job of this. Remember that a true master of the garden works a lifetime to develop not only the ability to garden but also the garden itself. How you place each stone is essential. It must come from a place of truth within yourself, each stepping-stone, each plant that is placed into the earth, each tree, the way the water is guided. One of the most important things to remember is that this work is really about the garden of your inner truth.

Take some time to build your garden just as you would like it to be.

Your garden is an art form like a painting. It will express so much more than your words could ever express. One of the most sacred aspects of your sacred garden is a certain stone that has a Buddhist-like name, the Absolute Control Stone. Its purpose in your garden is to be a guardian. When that Control Stone is set properly, it will bring good fortune. If it is in the wrong place in your garden, it will not bring good luck to you. A Control Stone that is set properly helps your prayers to be answered. It helps keep out darkness and evil from your garden. It controls the area and makes it powerful for you and helps you to manifest your dreams into being.

Think of a stone that has a strong color, an authoritative color, a color that you cannot help but notice. Think of a stone that has a presence. Formulate that stone within your mind. Walk around it. Find it in a place, perhaps, in the wilderness of your own mind, and bring it back to your gourd garden and set it properly. This should take some time. You walk around the interior of your gourd garden, remembering the position of the stars, getting a feeling of the landscape, positions of power, places of power within it, and then place your guardian stone, your Control Stone, from a strong vantage point.

I will give you several minutes to do this.

Now that you have found your Absolute Control Stone, the Reverence Stone, or Reverence Rock, is also very important to find. It is from where you place this rock that you observe your work of art, which is your garden. It is from this position that you observe the rest of the garden at all times. It is from there that you pray with the garden and let it teach you its wisdom. So the Reverence Rock is a more peaceful rock. It is a rock that you can pray near to or on, if you wish. Most people sit beside the rock. This Reverence Rock should probably be black, because it's about going inward, praying and dreaming. But it is also a stone that is a place of observation, so it has to be able to be in a position where you look across the garden and see all of it.

Now I'm going to give you some time to find a stone that fits that description, something that you feel very proud of. It's a proud stone and a powerful stone and should inspire admiration and beauty. Place it in your garden differently and yet corresponding to the Absolute Control Stone.

Take some time.

Now that you have found these two very important stones, I'd like you to take a minute or two and observe the feeling, the body of your garden, as if it were the body of a loved one. Caress it with your eyes, with your sensibilities. Be aware of the balance that is created within it. Let that balance bring harmony to your own soul. Allow the spirit of the garden to enter you in a quiet way. Feel the breeze on your skin. Hear the water and the birds. Smell the scent of flowers, or pine, or whatever trees you have in your garden. Make that garden part of you, and be sure that you notice your world of silence and inner freedom that is this garden. Notice that there are irises. What color are the spring flowers? What is the fragrance in the air? Allow yourself to move into the tranquility that is there, that is always there for you, now and in the future.

Take some time in your gourd garden.

Now that you have honored your garden, I would like you also to honor the spirit of the garden. There is a keeper of this garden. Perhaps this keeper will take form for you, or perhaps not. Perhaps it chooses to stay in spirit form in the form of energy. I'd like you to breathe deeply now and simply experience the spirit of your garden, the spirit deep within the reality of your sacred gourd.

Take some time.

Now that your garden is complete—and remember that, even if you don't see it exactly—allow yourself to sense it, to feel it, allow yourself to enjoy it.

Gourd Woman, who has a wonderful smile and a sense of humor about it all, walks with you down the paths of your garden. You walk together, looking at the flowers and the sacred herbs, perhaps the trees. You run your hands along the bark of the trees. You hold the stones, perhaps, in your hands. Maybe you kneel next to the water, touching your hands to the surface of it, causing an eddy of circles, of little ridges, to move out farther and farther into the center of the pond. You see a serene and peaceful beauty here that represents the garden of your own spirit. It is a place of serenity within your life, within your busy day, where you can go and commune with Gourd Woman. She is a good teacher for you. She will sit by the water and teach you endlessly if only you ask, but you must bring her energy as well. You must give her your love and send her light with your intent and your heart.

For a moment sit by the side of the water, which is like a mirror that you have created. And closing your eyes, create a beautiful light aura of green and golden light around Gourd Woman.

Take several minutes.

Now Gourd Woman surrounds you with a lavender light of higher consciousness. She touches you gently on your heart with a sprig from the sacred thistle bush that grows nearby, and she says, "Open your heart to all of the existence of life. Allow yourself to experience the beauty of nature, the balance of nature, as if it were your own, and know that when you are out of balance, you are creating imbalance in your universe, in all of nature around you. Understand the teachings of the gourd, and walk in beauty."

She gets up and slowly walks up the ladder out of the gourd. You see the universe, the night sky, above you with a twinge of orange light streaking the horizon, and you know that dawn is coming. You see Gourd Woman disappearing into the night, and as you watch the moon, you see her reenter her domicile—the full moon near the horizon. And she is gone.

You take a deep breath, and for a moment you say a prayer for your garden within the gourd.

Take a moment.

Now that your prayers are over, you bless this beautiful garden of your own serenity and peace. You walk up the ladder carefully each step of the way until now you are outside the gourd again, holding it against your belly with your arms around it in a position of comfort and happiness. Then slowly the gourd disappears and moves back into spirit. You take a deep breath and you begin to reenter the room.

Take several deep breaths, wiggle your toes and your fingers, and the rest of your body. Slowly and very carefully come back into the room opening your eyes as it feels comfortable.

Take a moment to write in your journal.

◆ ◆ ◆ ◆ ◆ WORKSHEET ◆ ◆ ◆ ◆ ◆

Remember and describe in detail your garden.

What marked the focal point of your garden?

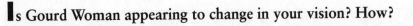

Is Gourd Woman appearing to change in your vision? How?

Did you feel power from your Absolute Control Stone?

WOMAN OF POWER

SACRED WHEELS

❖ ❖ ❖ ❖ ❖ ❖ ❖ ❖ ❖ ❖ ❖ ❖ ❖ ❖ ❖ ❖

The Self-Worth and Power Woman sacred wheels are aspects of the teachings of Woman at the Edge of Two Worlds, who is an archetype, a goddess figure who stands at the gateway between the first world—the first ring of power in a woman's life—and the second world. The first world is dedicated to physical existence: the raising of a family, acts of power that have to do with career, choices in relationships, and dealings with conditioning of family and society. At the second ring of power—the second world into which a woman is initiated by Woman at the Edge of Two Worlds—the great goddess provides a bridge for a woman's voyage to the enlightened, sacred life that marks the second half of her evolution.

Women the world over are struggling to understand the true meaning, the essence, of their lives. I have experienced with my teachers, Agnes Whistling Elk and Ruby Plenty Chiefs, that the feminine rites of passage are gateways into the sacred mysteries of a woman's existence on earth, times when she can discover the deeper meaning she has sought. And yet, these rites of passage are usually silent, unmentioned and mysterious journeys.

At the nucleus of the sacred rites of the feminine are the sacred wheels that help each woman discover her own personal mystery and illuminate her private relationship to the totality of her own life process. As she develops, she begins to choreograph the energies of the universe in a very new way. Every woman experiences and expresses this new understanding of self and sacredness differently. This experience can be profoundly strengthening and full of joy. To ensure such a positive effect, each sacred rite of passage in a woman's life needs to be fully illuminated so that the actual event becomes the beginning of a new and beautiful way of life.

These wheels are about the sacred rites of the feminine. They are about the uses of the energy that all women possess and how to use this energy in relation to your universe and to the spiritual and sacred aspect of your being. In working with these wheels, you will be reintroduced to the deep, internal beauty that comes with age—the beauty that makes itself visible by virtue of its innate power. As you feel this beauty, you will express it, and all those with whom you come in contact will be touched by your newfound strength, your heightened awareness, and the loveliness that emanates from deep within you.

In most sacred teachings in the world there are secret keys that make the teachings work like magic. Without the keys, the teachings can become knowledge, but never wisdom. They become the difference between information and experience of truth. When a key is given to you if you handle it properly, it changes you. When that change occurs, a space is created between the known ground where you have always lived and unknown territory. It is within that space that a true relationship with life is born. I present to you sacred wheels for you to work with through the coming year. The Sisterhood and I designed the wheels as a result of the needs and the dynamic energy of the women I have worked with through the gateway of wise-blood.

The wheel entitled Self-Worth is a wheel that involves inner searching or an implosion of energy. Sit in the center of an actual wheel that you construct or a wheel in your mind. A partner can work with you by sitting in the four different directions as you move around the wheel. A partner helps you hold the "power" of a direction and keeps you honest with yourself. When you finish, your partner changes position with you. The most important experience of this wheel is taking in energy, or an implosion of energy. Experience that feminine use of energy to its fullest.

The next wheel, Power Woman, acts as the key for both wheels by being a reversal of energy, or an explosion of energy, as a celebration of what you have found to be the core energy of your expression of power as a woman. Without the celebration, the Self-Worth wheel goes dormant. Do the Self-Worth wheel many times, and then move on to your Power Woman wheel. These can be done over and over to center yourself and to help you grow through each passage in your life. They are invaluable, as you will see, as tools for your path of empowerment.

WOMAN OF POWER   SELF-WORTH

SPIRIT LODGE

AM I WORTHY OF SUCCESS?
DO I DESERVE COSMIC POWER?
DO I LIVE MY SPIRIT TRUTH?
RETRIEVE YOUR SPIRIT NOW.

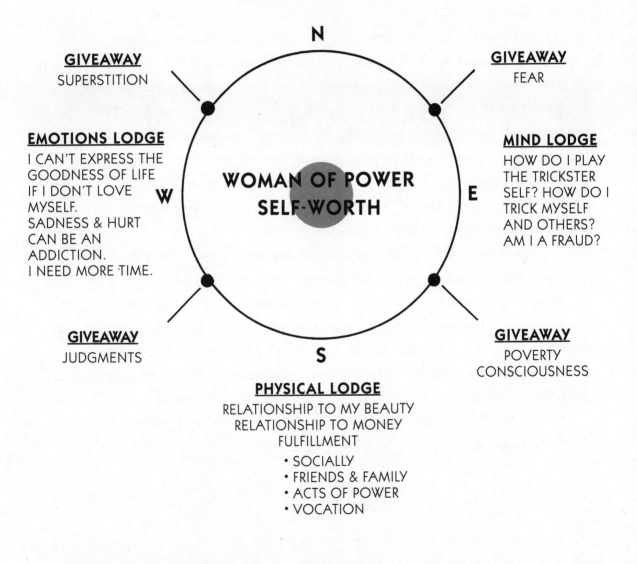

GIVEAWAY
SUPERSTITION

GIVEAWAY
FEAR

N

EMOTIONS LODGE

I CAN'T EXPRESS THE
GOODNESS OF LIFE
IF I DON'T LOVE
MYSELF.
SADNESS & HURT
CAN BE AN
ADDICTION.
I NEED MORE TIME.

W

**WOMAN OF POWER
SELF-WORTH**

E

MIND LODGE

HOW DO I PLAY
THE TRICKSTER
SELF? HOW DO I
TRICK MYSELF
AND OTHERS?
AM I A FRAUD?

GIVEAWAY
JUDGMENTS

S

GIVEAWAY
POVERTY
CONSCIOUSNESS

PHYSICAL LODGE

RELATIONSHIP TO MY BEAUTY
RELATIONSHIP TO MONEY
FULFILLMENT

• SOCIALLY
• FRIENDS & FAMILY
• ACTS OF POWER
• VOCATION

THE GIVEAWAYS ARE PERFORMED AS PRAYERS OUT LOUD TO THE GREAT
SPIRIT AND THE GREAT MOTHER AND GOURD WOMAN.

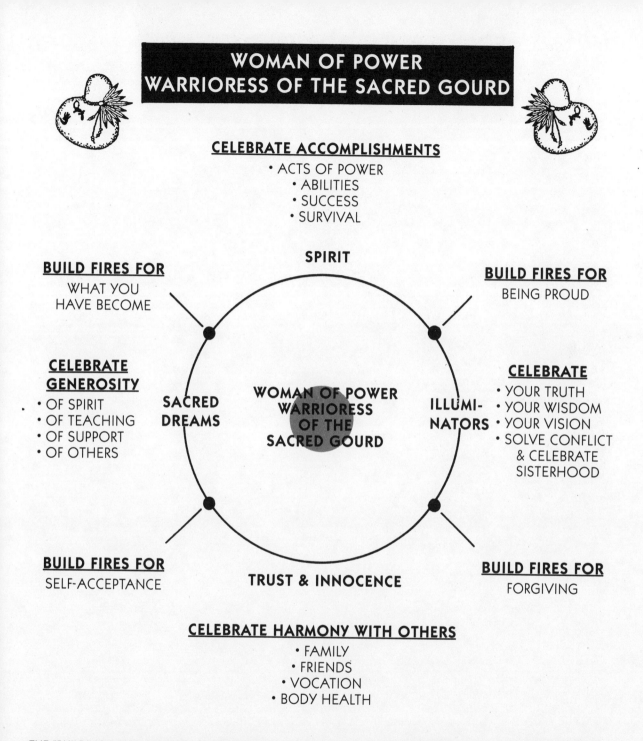

WOMAN OF POWER
WARRIORESS OF THE SACRED GOURD

CELEBRATE ACCOMPLISHMENTS
- ACTS OF POWER
- ABILITIES
- SUCCESS
- SURVIVAL

SPIRIT

BUILD FIRES FOR
WHAT YOU
HAVE BECOME

BUILD FIRES FOR
BEING PROUD

**CELEBRATE
GENEROSITY**
- OF SPIRIT
- OF TEACHING
- OF SUPPORT
- OF OTHERS

SACRED
DREAMS

WOMAN OF POWER
WARRIORESS
OF THE
SACRED GOURD

ILLUMI-
NATORS

CELEBRATE
- YOUR TRUTH
- YOUR WISDOM
- YOUR VISION
- SOLVE CONFLICT
  & CELEBRATE
  SISTERHOOD

BUILD FIRES FOR
SELF-ACCEPTANCE

TRUST & INNOCENCE

BUILD FIRES FOR
FORGIVING

CELEBRATE HARMONY WITH OTHERS
- FAMILY
- FRIENDS
- VOCATION
- BODY HEALTH

THE "BUILDING FIRES" CONDUCT A REVERSAL OF ENERGY FLOW FROM THE PREVIOUS GIVEAWAYS, E.G., FROM IMPLOSION YOU MOVE TO EXPLOSION AND THE SACRED DANCE OF MOVEMENT IS BORN. IN MOVEMENT IS THE CREATION OF LIFE AND ENLIGHTENMENT. YOU CAN LIGHT A CANDLE FOR THE FIRE OR BUILD A FIRE OR USE A FIREPLACE. WRITE ON A PIECE OF PAPER WHAT YOU ARE PROUD OF, ETC. DANCE YOUR FEELINGS OF CELEBRATION AND THEN BURN YOUR PAPER WITH THE WRITING SO YOUR MESSAGES ARE TAKEN TO THE GREAT SPIRIT & GOURD WOMAN. VISUALIZE YOURSELF STANDING IN THE CENTER OF YOUR OWN TRUTH AND INTEGRITY.

FREEDOM

FINDING THE INNER TRUTH
THAT SETS YOU FREE

Witness

Live in your sacred witness. That inner place of silence and observing is your true identity and therefore your true power. It is all you really have when all else is gone. Like monoliths in an ancient valley, the great stones observe and remember the passage of the ages. The answers that you find through the timelessness of spirituality and the innocence of nature offer the infinite. Each human being is on his or her own path, each different from yours. Answers to your questions are rarely found in another human. Answer your own questions by reflecting on nature and conversing with your own sacred witness. Rocks like the Pyramids or the stones on Easter Island are a testimony to time gone by, to the oceans of consciousness and unconsciousness that have existed before us. The stone monuments also represent the human in the passage of time and the universality of truth that is held within Mother Earth. It is important to learn to stand still, in silence, in the sacred witness within you. Meditate on stones and the great rock formations that have lived through the ages. Move into the essence of those stones. Through the stillness you become aware of, you will begin to experience the sacred witness that lives inside you. Listen to your heart, because the sacred witness is, in the end, all that you have, but it takes great wisdom and illumination to become your sacred witness.

—The Power Deck

CAVE OF THE DREAMING GOURD

HEALING RELATIONSHIPS

✦ ✦ ✦ ✦ ✦ ✦ ✦ ✦ ✦ ✦ ✦ ✦ ✦ ✦

Introduction

Many people become uncomfortable when you talk about other levels of consciousness, even about meditation or visualizations. They think that these are practices that are for Buddhists in monasteries in the Himalayas, certainly not relative to your everyday life. But I think through my own experience I can say that we are very fortunate to have this magnificent instrument—the human body. This body can be used as an antenna. It can bring in impulses from the stars, up from the earth, and from other levels of consciousness within our own universe, within our own world. You have the ability to live a very powerful and a very magical life that is full of freedom instead of restriction. You can lead a life where you can manifest your dreams and understand the true meanings of time. Time is something that you can learn to use, instead of being used and ravaged by time.

Ceremony/Meditation

I'd like you to take a deep breath. Close your eyes. Breathe from your belly. With each breath that you breathe in, visualize golden light, golden beautiful light, coming in and filling your body with warmth and comfort. As you breathe out, see the color green. Green is the energy of the heart, of self-acceptance. Breathe out green light. Breathe in golden light and breathe out green light.

Center yourself, understanding that your left side is female and your right side is your male. The male side is more aggressive, moving out into the world. The left side is female—more receptive, more creative, more intuitive. Keep breathing. Settle yourself into your center, into your place of power that lives around your navel, around the navel area, the solar plexus, and below.

This meditation is to help you exercise "muscles" in your brain and in your will that perhaps you have not used before. When I say "muscles," I am saying that the brain, like any other part of your body, needs to be exercised and tuned to be of any real use to you.

So, follow me. Move into the center of my words, and if you can, lay aside the problems of your day, doubts that you may have, because we all doubt. There's nothing wrong with doubt, because you don't want to be fooled in life. You want to move into the center of your own truth. So come along on this journey. We are extraordinary women, moving through our various passages in life, and we want to understand these passages. We want to understand who we are as women, not only in the society that we live in, which is very important, but also in the sense of the more cosmic, universal consciousness that we originate from.

...

Take another deep breath. Let everything go.

You are in a sacred place now, where you are safe and loved and cared for. Let yourself have these feelings as you begin to see a wilderness setting. This wilderness setting is near the ocean in a mountainous area. Snow-capped mountains surround you, but it is summer, and you are very comfortable. It's not too warm; it's not too cold.

You are walking down a trail, feeling the earth beneath your feet and smelling the cedar trees nearby. You are very thoughtful this day. You are thinking about your life, thinking about the many things that you don't understand and wish that you had answers for. You think a lot about rites of passage and how sad it is that we as a society have chosen to ignore traditions that celebrate passages. You feel, perhaps, proud of yourself. You would like to celebrate what you have become. I am sure that, like all people, you feel sad about other things that you have not accomplished, things that you would have liked to have done if you'd had the opportunity.

As you walk along, you're thinking these things, and you see up ahead of you what looks like an ancient ceremonial site. There are old stones set in circles. There are carvings on ancient stelle, stonelike reliefs of goddess figures. As you look around this area, fascinated that you have never heard of it before, you become aware of the scent of the ocean in the air, and again the smell of pine and cedar. Your heart fills with a kind of joy at being in the presence of such an ancient ceremonial grounds. You wonder about the culture that built it.

As you walk, still on your path, you see a hole in the ground and a ladder sticking up out of it. Of course, you cannot simply walk by.

You go over to the hole, and you look down inside, and you see very far down in the distance what looks like a fire, like flames dancing in the darkness. There is the smell of cedar wood in the air.

You follow your intuition, and you begin to climb down the ladder. As you do so, you sense that your life is going to change forever in a very good way. You know that something good is about to happen. You go down the ladder, one step after the other. You reach the bottom, and step off the ladder into a high-vaulted room carved out of stone. You look around as your eyes adjust to the darkness. There is a small fire burning. Sitting next to the fire is an old wise woman. She is very beautiful. You can see in her eyes a great history of life. She's wearing red. A red, beaded shield hangs around her neck. She wears her hair back, tied at the nape of her neck, and she is sitting, holding what you think at first is a basket. Then you realize that it's a very large gourd with many symbols painted on the outside.

"You are welcome here." The woman speaks to you very gently. "I am Gourd Woman," she says. "There are many things you need to know. I am the keeper of the sacred gourds, and the gourds represent the sacred void. Woman carries the sacred void. It has always been that way. The teachings of the sacred gourd can be yours now, because you are woman, and they are part of who you are in this lifetime. The sacred wheels of the sacred gourd teach you, as a woman, how to live, how to understand the rites of passage that we as women all move through in a lifetime. They teach you that we are part of a greater puzzle, part of a universe beyond our wildest dreams. The sacred gourd is like the womb of the universe, and it is just like the womb that you carry now. Your womb is very sacred. When you move through the gateway of Woman at the Edge of Two Worlds, the gateway of menopause and wise-blood, you take the sacred gourd, the womb, outside yourself, and put it into the world in front of you as a sacred vessel in which you stir the magic of your life and your dreams. It is within this vessel that your dreams manifest into being, into the world.

"So you, as woman, must learn about the sacred gourd. Today I will teach you. I will teach you one of the sacred wheels. You will experience it, because just my words mean nothing to you. But if you experience these things, they become part of your dream and don't just live within me."

The old woman reaches out to you and asks you to come closer. You walk around the fire to where she sits. She motions for you to sit on the red sacred blanket. She sets the gourd between you.

"Here. You feel this," she says. "You take it. Hold it next to your belly, and you will feel her power."

You pick up the gourd, feeling it with your fingers. It feels almost like skin under the palms of your hands. You trace the beautiful designs that have been painted onto it, and you imagine that this is one of the oldest gourds that you have ever seen.

"Now take the gourd, and touch your forehead between your eyes—that's your shaman eye," she says.

You hold the gourd to your forehead, and you feel almost a pulse from within the gourd. It's as if the gourd is truly alive. Then the old woman tells you to hold it to your heart, which you do. You can feel the beating of your own heart, matching the vibration from the gourd itself, and you are thrilled. Then she tells you to hold it next to your womb. As you do this, you close your eyes, and for a moment you go back in time. You see in your mind's eye a ceremony, where there are women in sisterhood who love one another, that perhaps you were part of in ancient times. They are doing ceremony around a fire, and they are holding their gourds. There's a sweetness and a gentleness to them, and a humor. It brings tears to your eyes.

When you open your eyes, Gourd Woman is standing before you. It is as if, without realizing it, some time has passed. She asks you to set the gourd down and to stand. She takes you by the hand and leads you to a room off to the left of this central room. She takes you to the doorway but does not go inside with you.

She says to you, "You will be doing ceremony soon, but before you do ceremony, it is important that you prepare yourself. I can see that you have certain problems or difficulties or tension with someone in your life or your family. I want you to enter the room, and you will see a shield in front of you. It will be blank. There will be red paint near the shield, and I want you to write on the shield, on the side facing you, the feeling that you have when you think about this person, particularly the tension that is troubling you. In other words, if you are having trouble with your father, you might put down the feeling 'unloved' or 'confused' or 'angry.' And then on the other side of the shield, which is also blank, write the feeling that you wish you had with this person—'joy' or 'communication' or 'humor,' whatever it is that you wish you had with that person.

"So now I send you into this room. I will wait for you by the fire."

You enter this very dark room, moving around in the darkness, trying to see. You move to the right and you see a candle burning, and then you see the shield. It is hung with eagle feathers and bright red ribbons. You move over to it, and taking the red paint, you write down the word that describes the feeling that you need to resolve.

If you have nothing to resolve with your family, then think of someone close to you.

Take some time.

Now that you have written this feeling on one side of this shield, move to the back side of the shield to the feeling that you would like to have with this family member or person if the conflict were resolved.

Take some time.

Now that you have written these feelings on your shield, you walk out of the room. Gourd Woman is waiting for you. She says nothing, but she takes you across the larger room to another small space.

This time she says, "When you enter, I want you to sit on the great stone chair and visualize meeting the family member or person that you have been thinking of. Visualize a conversation that is normal for the two of you, with all of its pain, with all of its emotion, whatever that may be. Visualize that situation as it is. When you are through, leave the room, and I will be waiting for you."

Take some time.

Now that you have met with the person and met with the difficulty, the old woman says, "I will take you to the next room. In this room you will find an altar. I would like you to sit before the stone altar and light a candle and smudge yourself with incense from the central container burning there. Smudge yourself, cupping your hands and bringing the smoke over your head and your body to bless and purify your energy field. Visualize this relationship with your family member or people in your life as you would like it to be, giving you the emotion that you wrote on the back side of your shield.

"Go now. I will wait for you."

You move into this room and see an altar lined with candles and prayer sticks. Beautiful goddess icons line the edge of the room. You go before the altar, and you sit on a stone that is set there. This time you take time for yourself and visualize the situation as healed, as deeply rewarding as you can imagine it to be.

Give yourself some time.

Now that you have accomplished this, you move out of the room to where Gourd Woman is waiting for you. In her hand is a small gourd, which she hands to you.

"Here, my child," she says, "is a dreaming gourd. Take it with you and dream with her. Begin to understand the first teachings of the sacred gourd. Begin to take your power in this lifetime. And now, let's sit again in front of the fire. I want to speak with you."

You sit with the old woman, feeling very close to her even though you have just met her. She is a warm, magnificent woman with extraordinary grace and wisdom.

"I know that there are certain things in your life that you wish that you had done," she says, holding her hand out and touching your shoulder. "I know that you would so much like to have, perhaps, lived some aspects of your life differently—such as have a child or get a divorce or get married or be in a different profession. But the circumstances were not correct for you to do whatever it is that you wanted to accomplish and somehow never could—because of the circumstance, because of your own lack of courage. I would like you to tell me about it now, because I can help you greatly to move on and find a better way. This is my gift to you."

The light from the fire dances in her eyes as she leads you into the east room, which is empty. You sit in the center across from Gourd Woman. The luminous darkness of the room helps you to feel your own serenity and power.

"I can help you to manifest your dreams as you truly want them to be. Tell me of your dreams," the old woman says. "Take some time and speak to me openly, now, as I place the old grandmother gourd between us."

I'll give you a moment.

Gourd Woman thanks you for your trust in her, thanks you for speaking with her. She looks at you with tremendous intensity in her eyes and says, "True power is in gentleness. It is important for you to understand this as a young woman of power. Now, I say young, because even if you have lived over half a century, you are still young in your work with me.

"The sacred wheels are important in your life, and I have shown you just now in the rooms off of the sacred fire an aspect of the sacred wheel. Sacred wheels are a way of teaching you about yourself. They are a way of bringing you closer to your own enlightenment. Sacred wheels are always set in the four directions. Without knowing it, you have moved from the south to the north and from the west to the east in the sacred rooms.

"By making an effort, by putting something out into the world into expression, you learn something about yourself. The wheels are about that, about give and take—putting out into the world something, creating a mirror that you can look into, and unavoidably you will see the truth reflected there. Perhaps that truth is positive and makes you proud. Perhaps that truth is negative and makes you realize that you have a lot yet to learn. And that's wonderful, because you're in this life to learn. This life is about enlightenment, and yet it is the one thing that you are probably most afraid of, because it speaks of the unknown and perhaps change. That's hard for all of us to face. But we are living in a time when change is inevitable, so you may as well get used to it," Gourd Woman says with a hint of humor in her eyes as she watches you.

"I understand," you tell her.

She smiles and says, "Yes, I know that you do. And I know that even though change is frightening to you that you are willing to make those changes if you believe that they are necessary and if you see what is necessary. I am here to help you with this, and the sacred wheels are here in existence to help you understand who you are.

"So now, I send you up the ladder and on your way. But take your dreaming gourd with you, and one day after your ceremony paint the symbols of your own dream onto the skin of the gourd. The gourd, remember, is the womb of the universe and represents the sacred void, which you, like all women, carry. Guard her well and use her well, for she is your true friend."

Gourd Woman reaches out to you and gives you a hug. You hug her back and thank her for her wisdom. She sits back down by the fire.

You begin your journey up the ladder. It seems much longer this time. You step carefully, realizing that as you step up toward the light and out of the cave that you are stepping out of the subconscious and back into your conscious mind and everyday reality. When you reach the top, you look back down, holding your gourd to your belly. You look down into the cave, and the firelight has been extinguished. Gourd Woman is but a memory, as if she were a dream. You take a deep breath, knowing that you will see her again. You take another deep breath and let all of the images fade away, feeling lighter and happier now, and more centered within your own being.

Open your eyes when you feel comfortable. And before you speak to anyone, write in your journal about what you found in the cave of Gourd Woman.

◆ ◆ ◆ ◆ ◆ **WORKSHEET** ◆ ◆ ◆ ◆ ◆

Draw your shield. What symbol or word did you place upon it that represents your emotions? What is it that you need to resolve?

What are the symbols of your own dream in life that you will paint upon your dreaming gourd?

Who is the person who upsets you most in life?

Describe your most loving relationship.

CAVE (
DREAM
GOURI

109

DREAMTIME POWER ANIMAL

EXPERIENCE THE WILDNESS OF YOUR SPIRIT

✧ ✧ ✧ ✧ ✧ ✧ ✧ ✧ ✧ ✧ ✧ ✧ ✧ ✧ ✧ ✧ ✧

Ceremony/Meditation

You will need a partner for this meditation.

Join with your partner. Sit, holding each other's hands, and tell each other in your own way that you lend each other your energies during this journey. Many of us hold our spiritual experiences like a secret treasure, and that's beautiful. But the teachings of the sacred gourd and its celebration can also be done in pairs. Learning to share positions of power and your rites of feminine passage is a strong element within this teaching.

Take a moment.

When you lie down, be sure you touch your partner somewhere very gently. Always remember that real power is gentleness. Take a deep breath and get comfortable. You will not be interacting with your partner again. You are finding a power animal for yourself, not your partner, but you are sharing an energy field.

Lie down, close your eyes, take several deep breaths, and move deeply into a state of meditation. This is not meant to be a frightening journey. I want you to realize in your deepest self—that part of yourself that wants to become all-knowing and wise and a woman of power— that this journey we are about to go on is a journey back into your own primordial time, back into your own history as an intelligent human being. We are searching for your original nature, your dreaming power animal. This animal helps you to take your power while you dream so that your everyday life becomes stronger. This animal is also your ally and protector as you celebrate your rites of feminine passage.

To find your original nature, we have to begin to uncover your real self. Within your true self dwells your power. It is this power that we need to discover. We are going to travel back (down) into time to your beginnings.

During this dream, I want you to become aware, first of all, of your physical being—your skin, your flesh, your organs, your intestines, and the armature of your skeleton, your bones. Try and feel them. Take a moment to experience your stomach as distinct from your intestines.

(Pause)

Feel the fullness or emptiness of your stomach. Feel the energy movement in your intestines.

(Pause)

Now feel your heart beating. Take a deep breath, and sense the expansion of your lungs. Feel your ribs moving.

Let yourself go deeper.

Tense your leg muscles, and feel the muscles held in place by your leg bones. Realize how perfectly your body functions and how much you take it for granted. Realize how your organs and glands feed your flesh and clean your blood without your even thinking about it.

Take a deep breath.

Now I want you to let your consciousness wander through your body, looking for your true self—that sacred place of power, your original nature, that place within yourself, possibly your heart or your mind, where you feel most comfortable. Take just a moment, and when you find it, remember it.

(Pause)

You have come to power because you desire to see. Let power help you. Through the process of mind, we are going to journey into the Lower World, a place that has a great shamanistic value. I am going to provide you with the opportunity to experience your own transformation into what we call "original spirit nature," or your power animal form.

Your power animal is a force of energy that equates with your own primary nature. Your power animal could be a mammal, bird, fish, dolphin, even a dragon; but it is not ever a fanged creature that bares its teeth or any of the creepy-crawlies. If one of those beings presents itself to you in an ominous manner, turn away and go on. If it persists, simply come back up the tunnel and end the journey. Wait and take the journey another time.

Let your thoughts clear. Take another deep breath, and slowly relax your muscles completely. Let your thoughts empty out of your mind. Roll your eyes up in your head, and visualize golden white light emanating from your crown chakra at the top of your head. Breathe deeply, and rest in the golden light for a few moments, letting it surround you with its healing protection.

Visualize yourself in a wilderness setting. You are walking. Up ahead you see craggy mountains rising high above you. You notice that there are occasional clouds in the very blue sky. The sun is shining. It's a very beautiful, temperate day. You hear coming down from the heights of the mountains a tremendous, tumultuous flow of water. You hear it falling in what sounds like a magnificent fountain of waterfall. You begin to see this waterfall as you round a turn on the trail. You stand for a moment, transfixed by the beauty of the sun shining through the water and foam. It looks like crystals, tiny crystals, throwing prismatic reflections of rainbows into the mist all around. The sound is almost deafening as you walk toward the waterfall. You are guided by an inner voice that is telling you that this is a very sacred place, a place where many apprentices have journeyed before you.

As you enter the area of the waterfall, you look for a trail that is etched out of the stone wall, and you find it very quickly. Now the waterfall is creating such a deafening sound that you can hardly hear yourself think, and you progress on a rocky ledge underneath the waterfall itself. You look out from underneath the water that is sheeting over you, beyond you, into the sunlight. Beautiful colors of blue and pink and orange and red created by the sun on the water bring you into a tranquil feeling of peace and strength and quiet power.

As you move along the trail on the cliff, you come to a ceremonial cave that seems prepared for you. It is only a few feet above the surface of the pond at the bottom of the falls. You sit for a moment at the opening of the cave, getting your bearings and experiencing the power of this place.

Take a moment.

As you watch the waterfall and let its power merge with your own, you begin to feel strong and peaceful at the same time. You begin to feel an extraordinary sense of well-being. You take a deep breath, and you settle yourself more deeply into your place of power within your own being. You center your consciousness around your navel area, and again you take another deep breath.

As you sit in your own personal place of power, you view with excitement your own thoughts about the Lower World, the home of the ancestors and the power animals. You have, perhaps, visited the land of the power animals many times, but this journey is a different one. You are journeying deep within yourself within the world of power to the place of the power animals that will help you to focus in your feminine passage and your dreams in the coming year. This year is a focus of celebration. You are in a process of owning what you have become, owning your accomplishments, large or small, because in the eyes of the Great Spirit, every accomplishment in the light is a great accomplishment and furthers peace and the evolvement of spirit.

If you have other power animals in your life, take a moment to acknowledge those power animals and fleetingly see them in your mind's eye. If you have never received a power animal before, allow yourself to become prepared for the aspect of yourself that is the visualization of your true nature in the form of the power animal. Allow yourself to be open. Allow yourself to set aside doubt. Put doubt away from you. You can always pick up doubt like a book to be read at another time. Allow yourself simply to settle into the moment to the magnificent pictures that move through your mind, the magnificent pictures of magic and power that are there for you to see if only you will allow yourself to relax and become part of the moment. If you find yourself not seeing these visions too clearly, then feel them, because surely you can sense the presence of power all around you. Allow yourself to be bathed in that feeling. Allow yourself to be strengthened. Allow yourself to relax into the drumming and into the visualization that is to come.

As you sit at the edge of the cave, you look at the magnificent clouds above you, some of them thunderheads, dark, lined in gold, others white and puffy. The azure blue sky surrounds your universe like a luxurious blanket. You feel at one with the universe, and you know that power is your ally, that power is outside you and within you, that you are made of power. You are made of light. You are but an aspect of the Great Spirit. As you sit looking into the pond that is created by the tumultuous rapids falling above you and around you, you are taken into a place within yourself, a central place of magic as you watch the eddies on the surface of the water, the reflection of the clouds and the mountains around you. Soon you are very gently dreaming. The extraordinary power and noise and melody of the falls becomes part of the rush of energy that moves through your system.

And as you look into the water, you realize that there is no one else around. You take off your clothes and dive into the pool along with the waterfall. You dive deep beneath the surface. The water is warm and totally comfortable. In moments you realize that you can swim beneath the surface without the need for air. You find that you can breathe the water as if it were air. You're very excited as you dive deep below, looking at the configurations of the stones and the tiny bright fish swimming by.

As you swim you realize that you are beginning to move into a vortex of power, and it is circulating at a very fast rate. You allow yourself into this vortex, knowing that you are safe and protected and there is no other place in the world that you should be at this moment. You allow yourself to be taken by this energy. You just float, like a cotton cloud floating on the wind. You float, and you begin to circle in a sacred spiral down toward the bottom of the pond, but you are not frightened. You are not claustrophobic. There is nothing here that is meant to scare you. It is as if you are lying back into the arms of the Great Mother, and she holds you and rocks you and turns you gently, as if to put you to sleep for the night. As it happens, you move deeply into the dreamtime. Taking a deep breath, you allow yourself to go deeper and deeper along with the water, as it gently holds you and supports you and swirls you toward your destination.

Finally as you look around in the dimness of light, the golden glow from the sun so far above, you realize that you are in a tunnel that is spiraling down and down through the depths of time, through the depths of predestination and fate. You see a light at the end of the tunnel far below you, as you swirl gently down toward that light.

You find that the light is upon you, and suddenly, you are standing in a meadow. You look around and see that surely you are in the land of the power animals, for there are many animals grazing. There are birds flying above you, every kind of animal that you have ever known. And you walk through this meadow of flowers. It is a beautiful place, and surely, you think, it must be the place that animals come to in spirit. It is the place of the ancestors, of our ancestors and the ancestors of the great animals, the beings that give away so that we may live. And you know that as you walk through this beautiful meadow, that an animal or a bird, even a dolphin or a whale, is going to present itself to you. There are bodies of water in various places, so water creatures live there. You are either drawn toward the edge of the water, or as you walk, you move through the forest that is nearby.

The dreaming power animal that is yours, that is going to help you to clarify your position of celebration, your position in the world, the animal that is going to help you clarify your point of view as you move into the world, with your new gourd teachings, will present itself to you from four different sides. So you will see it front and back, and from either side. When that happens you will know that this animal is yours.

At that point, you will put your arms around this animal, and you will bring it over to the tunnel, and holding it you will take it gently up the tunnel with you until you are sitting at the side of the pond beneath the waterfall. When you put your arms around this animal, remember in the room to cross your arms physically over your chest. Crossing your arms over your chest lets your partner know exactly where you are. When you get up to the edge of the water to sit at the edge of the pond beneath the waterfall, then you will sit up in the room physically, so that your partner can see you and know where you are in your dreaming.

When the drumming stops, you will blow the breath of your spirit across the palms of your hands, envisioning your power animal. Then place your palms over your power center, breathing deeply, so that the spirit of the power animal enters into you and stays with you as long as you want him to live there. At that point, you will get up and you will dance your power animal.

Now take another deep breath as you walk through the meadows of the Lower World and continue to search for your power animal. I will leave you at this time. Remember to cross your arms over your chest when you put your arms around the animal. Take it up through the tunnel and to the side of the pond, at which time you will sit up.

When your power animal is found and within you, dance your power animal into being. Use the power of your visualization to give birth to your power animal into this life.

I send you blessings on your journey.

Describe your power animal. How did the power animal make you feel? How did the power animal feel about you?

Do some research on your power animal and write down all of its characteristics. Gain an intimate knowledge of the nature of your dreamtime power animal, its habitat, mating cycles, etc.

DO YOU FEEL FREE?

IN FINDING SPIRIT, YOU FIND FREEDOM

✧ ✧ ✧ ✧ ✧ ✧ ✧ ✧ ✧ ✧ ✧ ✧ ✧ ✧ ✧

Introduction

What is freedom? Years ago when I first met Agnes Whistling Elk one of the first things she asked me when we were sitting around her wooden table in her cabin in the far north of Canada was about that subject. She looked at me, watched me fidgeting beneath her gaze.

I finally looked up at her and said, "Why are you staring at me that way?"

She smiled, cocking her head to one side, and finally, she said to me, "What is it, Little Wolf, that keeps you from your freedom?"

I was surprised by her question, since we had just been talking about gourds and beading. I thought for a while, my mind a confused jumble of thoughts, and I felt inside myself a movement, a shift in perspective. I suddenly was looking at my restrictions from a different vantage point, and I told her so. "Agnes, that question brings up so many different reactions inside me that I suddenly didn't know exactly how to answer you. I have always thought of myself as free. After all, I live in a free country, so they tell me. And suddenly I didn't quite know what you meant, because, surely, I feel restrictions in my life, and those restrictions are mostly self-made."

Agnes nodded, agreeing with me emphatically.

"At first I think I would have said that what keeps me from my freedom are my responsibilities, and then I thought, Wait a minute. I have chosen my responsibilities because I have needed something. Is that right, Agnes?"

"Yes," she said, agreeing with me again. I remember a shaft of golden sunlight breaking through the thunderheads outside cast shadows across her face, moving as the clouds moved above us.

"But as I explore your question, I suddenly feel less and less free."

Agnes laughed and said, "Yes, Little Wolf, we put fences around our consciousness endlessly, maybe sometimes in the fear that we might be free." She looked at me very directly with her piercing gaze, again making me slightly uncomfortable.

I thought for a long time about freedom, and then I said, "Agnes, when I was raising my daughter, when she was a little girl, it became very clear to me that without restrictions, without limits in her life, she became very chaotic. At first I thought that was because she was just being a brat, and then I realized that she was searching for love, that limits somehow make one feel loved. So is it possible, Agnes, that we create limits in our lives to make us feel loved in some way?"

"When a person is very young, a child, and they're in the process of forming, learning how to think, learning how to approach the world," she said, "the limits are very important, because you are teaching that child how to bounce off the mirrors of life. You're giving them character. You're helping them to find a point of view in the

world, something that is so desperately important. And you hope you
are doing that not by imposing your own belief structures, but by
helping them to find their own. But nevertheless, when you are talking about an unformed child, it's very different from a person who is,
you hope, an adult in the world, although in terms of enlightenment,
we are still unformed children. So, yes, I think that people do place
many restrictions around their lives, fences if you will, but those
fences usually are born from the need for distraction, from the des-
perate need for noise in one's life. When we move from a place of
nothingness, emptiness, stillness, quiet, where the spirit can raise its
head and look back at us, we become scared, because we realize that
we are so empty. We are so used to having addictions, distractions,
endlessly, that we impose huge walls around our lives so that we are
constantly busy, constantly moving, constantly forging ahead, we
think, into a better life. But if you are forging ahead asleep, there is
nothing gained. For there to be real movement in your life, you must
first be awake, and to be awake, you must sit in the silence, in the
purity of your own being.

"So, again, Lynn, I ask you, What is it that keeps you from being
free?"

Tears came to my eyes suddenly as I realized that one of the greatest needs of my life has always been to be loved, and I would create
situations, active situations, where there were a lot of people around
and much activity, so I never had to experience the stillness of my
own spirit. It's one of the great lessons I've learned with Agnes—to
learn how to do that, how to sit still, how slowly to peel away the
addictions. One of my greatest fears in life is the fear of death, and
yet I know that life is a magnificent mystery and death is the flower-

ing of that life, the completion, the goal of this life, not something to be afraid of. And yet because it's a mystery, because it's something I cannot control, because it's the unknown, I'm still afraid. It's something that I will have to experience someday, as we all will.

Ceremony/Meditation

What I would like you all to do now is to take a deep breath and go even deeper. Get comfortable and let the troubles of the day move out of your mind, and again, listen to my words. Let them take you into the center of your own psyche, so that we can begin to dream together.

I'd like you to picture yourself in a wilderness place of your choice. Take a moment.

I want you to build a beautiful dreamlodge for yourself out of bent willows. Over the bent willows you have placed sacred blankets of all colors and all nations. It is high enough to stand in.

Take a moment.

See yourself inside of your dreamlodge. There is a central fire that keeps you warm. You are lying back on other blankets that keep you warm and comfortable. The most important thing is to forget your body so that you can be comfortable. And you are dreaming, and the question that is in your mind is about freedom, as we have been speaking of freedom.

(Pause)

...

I would like you to rise and sit in the west in the sacred circle around your fire. Look into the flames and watch them as they dance in the air. Think about your emotions and how they make unexpected movements like the flames. I would like you to ask yourself, What is it that is emotionally keeping me from being free?

Give yourself some time.

Now that you've discovered what is keeping you emotionally from being free, please get up and walk around the sacred fire to the north position. In the north is a white sacred blanket where you seat yourself. Closing your eyes, going very, very deeply, think about freedom in your life, how, perhaps, you've dreamed of freedom all of your life, particularly in your adult life. Think about how you've expressed yourself spiritually in your life. Ask yourself, What is spiritually keeping me from my freedom in this lifetime? And when you think of what is spiritually keeping you from your freedom, perhaps you might think of spiritual materialism. Spiritual materialism is when spirituality becomes like a possession, where you become so addicted to the process of what you think of as becoming spiritual that you lose all sight of what spirituality really means.

Go even deeper and take some time, thinking deeply about what is keeping you from freedom spiritually in your life.

Take some moments.

Now, if you would walk around the sacred fire to the east where there is a beautiful golden medicine blanket, I would like you to seat yourself, closing your eyes, and meditate in a sacred way. Think about what freedom means to you now that you've had a chance to think about it for a while. What is there in your life, what is there in your process of illumination, that place of the old wise one within you, that is keeping you from freedom? This could partly have to do with fear of retirement, where you know that you are going to have to have enough money later on in life. It may be part of what is keeping you so busy that you do not have time for your own being, for your own prayers, for the ceremony of spirituality. Also in the east, there is the mind. What is there in the mind, in your intellect, that is keeping you from your freedom? Is it the judgment, the doubting of your own strength and power? What are the mentations that you go through in a day that keep you from your spirituality?

Take some time.

Now that you have found what is keeping you mentally from experiencing freedom, please move to the south of the sacred fire, the position of the child, of trust and innocence, and sit on your red medicine blanket. This is a position of substance and physicality, how you take care of your body, how you take care of the physicalness in your world, how you take care of your family. It is the bedrock, the foundation of your spirit lodge. It is from this position that you go out to meet the world. It is from this position of the south. It is your trust and innocence. What is there in your physical life that is keeping you from freedom? Is there something in your life that keeps you in fear of movement, of moving forward? Are you always in stasis? Are you always moving backward, rehashing the old, not looking forward to the new?

I'd like you to take some time and discover what it is physically that is keeping you from your enlightenment.

Now that you have discovered the four directions of restraints that you have put around yourself, I'd like you to take the position, sitting, still, in the south, of the center of your sacred wheel. Open your

eyes now, and look into the fire. The fire sits in the position of the center of your sacred wheel. Think of yourself, for a moment, as that flame. As you look at the fire bursting with energy, golden, red, and blue light, think to yourself how is my freedom like this central fire?

Take some time.

I would like you to think, again, about being free. Closing your eyes now, think of all of the four directions and how freedom is like that fire within yourself. Thinking about freedom, I would like you to bring your consciousness down into that part of your body that experiences the thought of freedom. Where do you experience being free inside your body?

Take some time.

Now that you have located the feelings of freedom inside of yourself, look around in that location within your body, and see what form freedom takes. What does it look like? For me, freedom always looked like clouds floating over the mountains surrounding the desert. Freedom to me was being free on the wind. And then I learned much later in my life that you cannot be like a reed or a cloud in the wind, blowing this way and that, depending on the volition of the wind, but that there is an importance in having intent— for instance, the intent of wisdom, the intent of success. But within that framework, there is an enormous freedom—freedom to live, to enjoy what you have accomplished, freedom to celebrate who you are. So when you look inside of yourself to see the form of your freedom, take several minutes, and if you see yourself as a box or a cave, become that box or that cave. If you see yourself as clouds or the wind, become that wind with the clouds, and remember what it feels like to be that.

Take some time.

Now that you have felt your freedom from all of the four directions and from the center essence of your being, I'd like you to remember what you have found, so that you can write it in your journal before you speak to anyone.

Take a deep breath. Take another deep breath, and slowly as it feels comfortable, bring yourself back into the room. Take plenty of time.

WORKSHEET

What does freedom mean to you?

How do you take your freedom?

Do you have confusion over boundaries? How?

How do you see yourself?

CELEBRATION

TAKING STOCK OF WHAT YOU HAVE BECOME AND REINVENTING YOUR VISION OF LIFE

HUMOR

Humor, fear, and anger awaken the power of your will. In the juxtaposition of realities find truth, as in the primitive positioned in the wilderness of an urban setting. See how you have chosen your illusions, as others have, and seek to feel the laughter that holds together your daily dream. Self-importance blinds you to the source of joy and humor. Awaken the power of your will, and find your joy and your laughter. Awaken your sense of humor. Life is often surreal, with aspects of the primitive juxtaposed against the realities of our current civilized life. We need our sense of humor to remember that it is dangerous to be caught in the dream, to lose the understanding that the reality of life as we know it is only an illusion. One day we will awaken and understand what we have really come here to do. If we lose ourselves in self-importance and ego, we also lose our sense of humor and our understanding of truth and reality. Humor is part of your process toward illumination. Humor is of the mind, or in this case, perhaps, of losing the mind, setting the mind aside, and living in that state of humor that puts everything in perspective. Humor takes you back to your beginnings.

—The Power Deck

CELEBRATE WHAT YOU HAVE BECOME

RETRIEVING WHAT YOU HAVE DISOWNED

✧ ✧ ✧ ✧ ✧ ✧ ✧ ✧ ✧ ✧ ✧ ✧ ✧ ✧ ✧ ✧ ✧

These are directions for you to go out into a natural or wilderness setting in partners and to help each other celebrate what you have become, what you have accomplished in your lives.

Choose a partner. It doesn't matter whether you know this person or not, and perhaps one of you will be more experienced than the other. The one who is more experienced should be the first Listener. Go outside to some comfortable spot, and the first person, the Speaker, will tell her partner, the Listener, what she has accomplished in her life, what she has done, what her work is, what her family life is like, what it was like growing up. Each person should take a half an hour to relate this to the partner. As you talk, think of symbols for your accomplishments and draw them.

The big job is for the person who is listening. I want that person to move into her place of power, and together with her partner elicit from each other a sense of accomplishment in life. So, before you begin, close your eyes. Take a couple of deep breaths and move your center of power down into your navel to the shaman place of power. Allow yourself to feel your strength and your shaman ability and your vision.

The Listener is the one who helps you to define, in essence, what you have become in your lifetime. This sounds like a very large process, but really it isn't. It is easy in a way to look at what someone is not allowing themselves to own. Your partner might say, "Oh well, I wrote a book this year, but you know anyone could have done that. It wasn't much." And the person listening hears that person denying the tremendous accomplishment she has made and brings that denial up to her. In other words, you're a mirror for your partner, a helpful, gentle mirror, not a teacher yet. You listen carefully. Perhaps this person has seemingly smaller accomplishments. What you have accomplished is not smaller. It is simply different. Maybe she has gotten married and perfected her cooking skills, perfected her ability to help her husband become everything that he can become. Perhaps she has dealt with very difficult children in her married life. In other words, accomplishing something does not necessarily mean something huge in life—being on the cover of *Time* magazine. It is something that is important for that person, and those are the things that we are looking for. Many events we deny to ourselves—women in particular deny what they have accomplished. It's as if their accomplishments are never enough, as if they are not big enough to recognize and make something of. These are the things that the Listener really needs to pay attention to and help her partner see. This is essential to becoming a shaman healer.

When you have talked for half an hour, then you switch positions. The Listener becomes the Speaker, and the person who has been telling moves into her shaman place of power. Take a moment. Close your eyes, and take time to redefine your place of power within yourself, always around your navel area. Move into that place of vision and body-mind. Perhaps you've never experienced that in your life. Perhaps you've never really moved into that place of power when listening to someone else. This is not a place of judgment, but a position of heart. This is the beginning of being a shaman teacher, of being a shaman within your own life.

This is a time of celebration. This is a time of moving out into the world, acknowledging who you are, what you have become, acknowledging the beautiful and magnificent being that you are. You are a person who is living in this world with courage, with absolute power and who is proud of what you have done with your life. Acknowledge what you have accomplished and remember what you have seen, so that you can write it in your journals when you are finished.

OUTLINE OF CEREMONY

What to bring: notebook and pen/pencil; something to sit on.

Both participants have important roles:

The Speaker will talk about what she has accomplished in life, about her family life; about growing up, etc. There are no big or small accomplishments, only what they mean to you. As you speak you may want your notebook open to draw or write about any symbols that come to you.

The Listener moves into her place of power and becomes the "mirror" for her partner. You help your partner to define what she has become or accomplished in this life. You support her in seeing how she truly is living in this world with courage. Perhaps you've never really moved into that place of power when listening to someone else. This is the beginning of being a shaman teacher, of being a shaman within your own life.

Find a comfortable spot.
To begin, move into your place of power.

- Take a few deep breaths. Close your eyes.
- Move your center down around your navel to the shaman place of power.
- Feel your strength, your ability and shaman power.

Give thanks to the Great Spirit.
Speaker: Speak about what you have accomplished in life.

- What is your work; what is family life like?
- What was it like growing up?
- Respond as your partner guides you.

Listener: Stay in your place of power.

- Help your partner to see her truth.
- Is she denying her own accomplishments; her true value; her own beauty and magnificence?
- Does she acknowledge that she is living with courage; in balance, understanding and accepting her absolute power in her own life?

Take half an hour for each person to speak.
When both partners are done, give thanks. Take some time to write in your journals.

Describe your accomplishments.

How did you feel about your partner's accomplishments?

PURIFICATION OF THE WOMB AND THE OFFERING OF LIGHT CEREMONY

✦ ✦ ✦ ✦ ✦ ✦ ✦ ✦ ✦ ✦ ✦ ✦ ✦ ✦ ✦ ✦ ✦

First Day

Introduction

This is the ceremony where you go in partners out into nature with gourds, and together you do this ceremony, placing your gourds into Mother Earth to be retrieved the next day. You need red natural material to place the gourd on, and another piece of red material to place over the gourd. Sign your red material with your name. You need rattles or drums or both so that you can play for your partner when she is calling in her power animal.

This is a ceremony that requires concentration and focus because you and your partner are going out to find a power spot that you agree upon. There's a reason for this. It's much easier to find a power spot for yourself, and much more difficult to find a power spot in partnership. It's important to be able to work with someone else in

your sacred work. Partnership is so often part of the process of celebration, and you need to learn how to share what you discover.

Ceremony/Meditation

Go, walking quietly with intent, and find a power spot that you both
agree upon. Then sit in that power spot for a few minutes, back to
back, and go into your place of power around your navel, your
shaman center, and silently say a prayer of thanks to the Great
Mother and the Great Spirit for helping you find this place of power,
and ask them to be with you in your ceremony. This should only take
a short time. Then decide between you who is to find the north and
south marker stones, and who is to find the west and east marker
stones. Those four stones always go together—north and south, east
and west. Set out to find those marker stones. This should only take
a few minutes. You meet back at your power spot, and place your
stones in a circle large enough to sit within comfortably and to contain two gourds because, remember, you're both going to be using
this circle for ceremony. So make it at least ten to twelve feet across.

Having found and placed your marker stones, place your gourds in
the center of the wheel on their red material. Then the two of you
walk together, using your rattles or your drums gently. You walk
around sunwise, saying a prayer to bless and protect your circle,
something like, "I place an aura of divine love and protection around
this sacred circle so that we are protected from all harm." Then call
in the powers of the four directions, beginning with south.

Then one person sits outside in the south of the wheel with her
drum or rattle, and the other person enters by the east door, moves
into the center of the sacred wheel and begins to do her shaman

dance of power. The other person, sitting in the south, plays the drum or rattle for you while you are calling in your allies and your power. Then when you feel that the energy vectors are strong, you move into calling your power animal, the one that you received earlier in your work. Visualize your power animal coming to you and being part of you. Everyone calls their power animal in their own way. Now, simply dance your power animal, because the strength and stealth of your power animal is with you now. Keep envisioning your power animal and begin to dance your power animal, as your partner plays the drum or rattle for you. You dance your power animal as long as you need to feel the oneness of energy, a few minutes usually. As you dance ask your power animal to be present during your ceremony, to give you clarity and power, to bring wisdom and strength to your gourd, to your ceremony, as you give away light into the universe to Gourd Woman for being there for you.

You envision light coming from within your gourd during this ceremony, as if the sun had descended from the sky and taken up new residence within it. Then, as you sit in the center of the wheel, you pick up your gourd and hold it to your belly. You roll it clockwise around, over your belly, feeling the emptiness of it and the fullness of it, keeping your eyes closed as you do so. Then, continuing to hold your gourd in your lap, you face south. The purpose of this ceremony is to purify your own womb, the female aspect that lives within you. At this time I want you to breathe deeply for a moment and center yourself. Then slowly take your consciousness down inside your womb. This is not inside the gourd as yet but inside your own sacred void. If you have had an operation or a hysterectomy, you still have the space within yourself that lives forever, because the etheric field is still there within you just as it always was. So go into that womb place inside you, and look around for a moment. Note the condition of your womb without judgment, but with love.

(Pause)

Now ask yourself, what traumas, what beauties and joy, what aspects of childhood, of early childhood before adolescence, still live within your womb that are perhaps keeping you from celebrating fully the femaleness that is within you out into the world. Take several minutes, moving inside yourself, quietly and silently, and remember.

Your partner holds the south position for you, and that means that your partner, sitting facing you, is holding the position of trust and innocence, physicality, physicalness, substance in the world. She is holding the strength of that position. She becomes the south and all that it means, and holds that position of power for you, lending her energy to you. She is very important in this ceremony. She visualizes the color red, of the south, and holds the power of trust and innocence with you.

So you ask yourself, What aspect of my needy child is keeping me from expressing my womanness, my femaleness, into the world? Or, if that is not the issue, perhaps you need to celebrate what you had in childhood. Celebrate to yourself how much nourishment you did receive in childhood. When you have found that, express it to your partner. Tell her what you have found—good or bad, frightening or joyous. The partner's position in this is to listen, unless she sees very, very definitely that something has been avoided. And if she sees that, she needs to mention it, but when she mentions it, it is simply a suggestion. She never takes the position of teacher. She only mentions it very, very gently, and that is all. And the person in the center can either take that into accord or not. That's really up to her, because this is really basically her ceremony. The position of the receptor, the person who is sitting in the position facing you is simply to lend you energy and power and to help you to find your own truth.

Then the person sitting in the center turns and faces the west. Your partner moves to the west position and holds the west position for you, visualizing the color of black obsidian, the position of adolescence, the position of the sacred dream, death and rebirth, transformation. And you, again, holding your gourd next to your belly, feeling it there at all times, ask yourself, What happened in my adolescent life that is keeping me from celebrating my femaleness into the world? What is it that I hold in my womb, what memories do I hold in my womb that I have not dealt with in adolescence? You do this silently, and when you find information, you tell your partner. If your partner senses something, she will share it with you. Take as long as you need for this.

Now you turn to the north, your partner moving with you, and you ask yourself, In the north what is it as an adult, what is it in my spirit and strength or wisdom that is keeping me from celebrating my femaleness, the beauty of my wombness into the world? And when you find what is living there, you tell your partner, who is holding north power and visualizing white like snow. Give her a chance to give you feedback if she feels that it's necessary. Again, the response should be very gentle, very quiet, not in a teacher mode, but as a very gentle suggestion. Remember it is your position in this particular ceremony to listen for the most part and hold the power of the direction.

Then you turn to the east, the position of mind and illumination and the color golden yellow. It is there that you ask the grandparents within you for guidance. You ask the grandparents what in your own wisdom is keeping you from expressing your femaleness into the world. Perhaps the fear of being devalued in some way, the fear of what fame could bring, keeps you from taking your power. How does your logical mind hold you back? That's just an example.

When you are finished discussing with your partner in the east, you hold your gourd up to Father Sky, and say a prayer to Father Sky for strength and power and guidance. Listen for a moment for his advice. Then hold your gourd down to Mother Earth and pray for guidance from the Great Mother to help you to understand what you do not see. Sit in stillness and listen for what comes to you. Then, when that is understood, and you have said your prayers, hold your gourd to your third eye, or shaman eye, and acknowledge to yourself and to your gourd that you have cleansed your own womb of personal history.

Then, holding your gourd back down again outside your interior womb, close your eyes and breathe deeply. Imagine that your own belly is merging with your gourd. Begin to experience the womb as if it has been moved into the gourd, not in the sense of flesh but in the sense of wisdom, that the gourd represents a cauldron of magic, a place for your brilliance, your talent, your creativity, and your power that can be created and celebrated. Begin to see the gourd as an exterior womb where all of your creativity can have a rebirth in a more tangible and meaningful way, so that you move into life with new energy and strength. Visualize brilliant golden sunlight and the sun high above you in the sky. Feel the sun on your face with your eyes closed. Take several deep breaths. Imagine this magnificent sun lending you its fiery light, and feel that sun moving down through the top of your head, down, down through your heart, filling your heart with love and light, moving down into your stomach, and eventually into your womb. Then see that light moving back out into your gourd, filling your gourd with golden light and all the colors of the rainbow. See your gourd filled with light. It is part of you, and yet it is an entity unto itself, a receiver, a sacred receiver, that will be there for you. It is a "talking bowl" for sharing wisdom with the Great Mother and the people you love. It contains a mirror for all that you are. It is a cauldron for magic and power. It is a place that mirrors your beauty and your comfort.

Then, digging a shallow indentation in the earth and covering the hollow with your material, you place your gourd back on the red piece of material, and then cover your gourd respectfully with the other square of cloth, and settle it down in the four corners with small stones while blessing it. Then you leave the sacred circle by the east door. Picking up your drum or rattle, you sit in the position of the south, facing your partner, as she takes her place in the center of the circle. And she repeats the ceremony that you have just created. Remember that now you are holding the position of the four directions. You lend her your power and strength, and you listen carefully. Shamanize your partner, and be aware of the shift in energy from your first position. You move from active to receptive. Help your partner to find her way to the center of her own sacred circle.

When your partner has finished her ceremony, you enter the circle by the east door, and sit back to back with her. Again, silently, give thanks to the Great Mother and to the Great Spirit. Send light into the universe to Gourd Woman, Keeper of the Sacred Gourds. When you are finished, leave the circle by the east gate. Then, take a pinch of tobacco and some cornmeal, and walk around that circle sunwise, again protecting the circle as you did before. Protect it from all harm. Then leave the circle behind, always remembering, however, to leave a marker. You have signed your red material with your name. Find your way back to camp, always walking with intent, but this time your intent is to celebrate a ceremony beautifully created.

PURIFICATION OF THE WOMB AND OFFERING OF LIGHT

What to bring: your gourds, two red cloths with your name on them, a rattle and/or drum, tobacco and cornmeal for blessing the circle, something to sit on.

Find a power spot for both of you with your partner. It's important to work together in your ceremony.

Sit back to back: move into your shaman center and offer a prayer of thanks.

Gather stones: one partner gathers north and south stones and the other gathers east and west stones. Both gather four smaller rocks.

Build a circle you can both sit and move in (about ten to twelve feet across). Place your gourds in the circle with the smaller rocks and red cloths.

Working together, you both move around outside of the circle with rattles/drums. Bless the circle and call in four directions.

Begin ceremony.

One person—Outside Voice—sits outside the circle, in the south, with the rattle or drum.

- Play for your partner as she dances.
- Send energy to her for her ceremony.

First person inside the circle—Inside Person

- Enter by east door.
- Call in and dance your power animal.
- Ask your power animal to be present, to give you clarity and power, and to bring power and strength to your gourd.
- You give away light to Gourd Woman.
- See light coming from your gourd.

Outside Voice sits in the south of the circle.

- Hold this position of trust and innocence, physicality and substance in the world.
- Send south energy to your partner in the place of listening on the inside of the circle.
- Make gentle suggestions only when absolutely necessary.
- Allow Inside Person to find her own truth.

Outside Voice gives these instructions to Inside Person to allow time for process:

- Sit in the center.
- Face south and hold gourd to your belly.
- With eyes closed, roll gourd clockwise over your belly.
- Sense its emptiness and fullness.
- Hold gourd in your lap.
- Move your consiousness into the place or space of your womb.

- Ask yourself what traumas, beauties, joys, and aspects of childhood you hold.
- Ask yourself what still lives within your womb that may keep you from fully celebrating your femaleness.
- Remember to celebrate what you had as a child.
- Take some time and then tell me what you see.
- Speak about what you've learned from the teachings of the south.

Inside Person turns and faces west.

Outside Voice moves to the west—the position of adolescence, the sacred dream, death, rebirth, and transformation.

Outside Voice give these instructions to Inside Person and allows time for process:

- Sit in the center.
- Face west and hold gourd to your belly.
- With eyes closed, roll gourd clockwise, over belly.
- Sense its emptiness and its fullness.
- Hold gourd in your lap.
- Move your consciousness into the place or space of your womb.
- Ask yourself what traumas, beauties, joys, aspects of adolescence you hold.
- Ask yourself what fears of death or transformation you hold.
- Holding your gourd, ask what still lives within your womb that happened in your adolescent life that keeps you from celebrating your femaleness.
- Remember to celebrate what you had as an adolescent.
- Celebrate your rebirth, your gifts from the sacred dream.

- Take some time and then tell me what you see.
- Share what you've learned from the teachings of the west.

PURIFICATION
OF THE WOMB
AND THE
OFFERING
OF LIGHT
CEREMONY

151

Inside Person turns and faces north.

Outside Voice moves to the north—the position of adult life, the place of spirit, strength, and wisdom.

Outside Voice gives these instructions to the Inside Person and allows time for process:
- Sitting in the center, face north and hold your gourd to your belly.
- With eyes closed, roll your gourd clockwise over your belly.
- Sense its emptiness and its fullness.
- Hold gourd in your lap.
- Move your consciousness into the place or space of your womb.
- Ask yourself what traumas, beauties, joys, aspects of your adult life you hold within your womb.
- What still lives within your womb that may keep you from celebrating your femaleness?
- Holding your gourd, ask yourself what has happened or is happening in your adult life that keeps you from celebrating your femaleness.
- Remember to celebrate what you have as an adult.
- Celebrate your spiritual path, your strength and growing wisdom.
- Take some time and then tell me what you see.
- Speak about what you've learned from the teachings of the north.

Inside Person turns and faces east.

Outside Person moves to the east—the place of illumination, the Old Wise One, the place of the grandparents within you where you ask for guidance, the place of the keepers of the ancients wisdoms.

Outside Voice gives these instructions to Inside Person and allows time for process:

• Sit in the center.

• Face east and hold gourd to your belly.

• With eyes closed, roll gourd clockwise over your belly.

• Sense its emptiness and its fullness.

• Hold gourd in your lap.

• Move your consciousness into the place or space of your womb.

• Ask yourself what traumas, beauties, joys, aspects of your Old Wise One you hold within your womb.

• What still lives within your womb that may keep you from fully celebrating your femaleness?

• Holding your gourd, ask yourself what ancient secret of fear keeps you from celebrating your femaleness.

• Remember to celebrate what you have as a wise one.

• Take some time and tell me what you see.

• Speak about what you've learned from the teachings of the east.

Outside Voice, holding energy in a sacred way and allowing the energy to move, gives the following ceremonial instructions:

• Now hold gourd and pray: up to Father Sky, down to Mother Earth. Sit in stillness, listen, and understand. Acknowledge that you cleansed your own womb of personal history.

PURIFICATION
OF THE WOMB
AND THE
OFFERING
OF LIGHT
CEREMONY

153

- Hold gourd next to your womb: experience your womb moving into the gourd. The gourd represents a cauldron of magic, a place for your brilliance where your power can be created and celebrated.
- Feel the brilliant golden sunlight on your head and face, giving you its fiery energy, moving down through your body, through your chakras, and then into your gourd.
- Place your gourd on a piece of red cloth, and cover it with the second red cloth. Anchor it with four small stones. Leave an offering. Bless it, and leave the circle by the east door.

Change places and begin again, repeating the full ceremony.

When complete, both enter the circle by the east door.

- Sit back to back.
- Silently give thanks.
- Send light into the universe to Gourd Woman.
- When finished, leave by the east door.

Working together:
- Walk around the circle sunwise, silently blessing the circle.
- Leave tobacco and cornmeal to protect the circle.

Return to camp.

What aspect of yourself is keeping you from expressing your woman-ness?

What was the prevailing ambiance of your childhood, prevailing mood, e.g., sadness, tension, carefree?

PURIFICATION
OF THE WOMB
AND THE
OFFERING
OF LIGHT
CEREMONY

155

Do you feel that way in your adult life?

PREPARING THE WOMB FOR MAGIC AND LIGHT

RETRIEVING YOUR GOURD FROM MOTHER EARTH

✧ ✧ ✧ ✧ ✧ ✧ ✧ ✧ ✧ ✧ ✧ ✧ ✧ ✧ ✧ ✧ ✧

Second Day

Introduction

You will perform this ceremony on the second day. You and your partner will return to your sacred circle to retrieve your gourds. You will need to bring your mirrors and a drum or rattle, something to make rhythm and music for your partner during the ceremony.

Ceremony/Meditation

You gather together and move out into nature with your partner to retrieve your gourds. As you are walking, talk about any dreams that you had that night. Talk about your feelings of the experience of the ceremony the day before. When you approach your sacred circle in the desert, become silent. Walk around your circle sunwise, blessing the circle with your prayers, first in the south, then to the west, then to the north, and then to the east. You can do this together in silence.

One person enters the sacred circle through the east door, and the other person holds the position of the south, of trust and innocence, of the sacred animals with their noses closest to the ground.

The person sitting in the center holds her gourd close to her belly. She closes her eyes, and facing her partner, she talks about what the inside of her womb feels like and is to her, perhaps what memories she feels are still there that need to be expressed. Talk about the sacredness of feeling female, being able to create into the world.

If you sit in the center now move your consciousness down into the sacred gourd and fill your gourd with golden light. Tighten your shaman center. Send your intent into your gourd, filling it with light and power and beauty. Know that you are creating a space for magic to happen, for the miracle of life to be created in a new way.

When you have completed your visualization, place your gourd back in the center, move out the east door and move to the south, taking your partner's place. She in turn moves to the center of the wheel. She picks up her gourd and repeats the visualization.

When she is finished, then both partners sit in the center of the sacred wheel, back to back, each holding her gourd in her lap. Take out your mirrors and hold the mirrors up to the sun, empowering them with the light of day and ask the moon to empower your gourds later on that night. Then place the mirrors inside the gourds. Then each of you at the same time, keeping your eyes closed, say a prayer to Gourd Woman. Thank her for being with you, for bringing you teachings and fulfillment of spirit. Then hold your gourd up to the sky and offer it to the sky fathers. Hold it down and offer it

to Mother Earth. Then turn your gourd around to the four directions in your hands, offering prayers to the four directions for guidance and strength and protection and power on your path. Then,
look into your gourd, and you will see the reflection of your own
eyes. Look into the reflection of your own eyes for a long time.
Take deep breaths, be still, and listen to the beat of your own heart.
As you look into the mirror, there should be a moment when your
own reflection leaves and there is a merging momentarily with God,
with a sense of the Goddess within you, and you feel the Great
Spirit permeate your being. That is the feeling that you are looking
for. That is the feeling, the merging, the oneness, the sense of oneness of all life. Continue to look in the mirror for a long time. It is
like a meditation. If you don't sense the merging, know that it will
come.

This is a meditation that I am going to want you to practice
throughout the coming year. When you are finished, say a prayer to
the Great Spirit, thanking the Great Spirit for the opportunity to do
this ceremony. Blessing your circle, taking the stones and returning
them to a natural environment, you leave this place of power and
head back to camp, carrying your gourds and your folded red
material.

OUTLINE OF CEREMONY
What to bring: mirrors, a drum and/or rattle, something to sit on.

Walk with your partner to your gourds. Talk about your feelings,
your dreams, and yesterday's ceremony.

Become silent as you approach your circle and pray.

- Walk around the circle sunwise.
- Bless your circle, starting in the south.
- Work together in silence.

Inside Person enters the circle by the east door and sits in the center.
Partner holds the south position.

Inside Person holds her gourd to her belly.

- Close your eyes.
- Talk about what the inside of your womb feels like.
- Talk about your memories.
- Talk about the sacredness of being female and being able to create in the world.

Inside Person moves her consciousness into the gourd.

- Fill it with golden light, power, and beauty.
- Create a space for magic to happen.
- When done, move out of the circle by the east door.

Change places with your partner.
Repeat the ceremony.
Both sit back to back in the center of the circle, holding gourds.

Place mirror inside gourd.

- Close your eyes.
- Together, in silence, say a prayer to Gourd Woman.
- Offer gourd, with your prayers, to Father Sky, Mother Earth, and the four directions.

Look into your gourd.

- See the reflection of your own eyes.
- Move into the oneness, merging with the God within you. Sense the Goddess.
- Spend time in this meditation.

In conclusion, say a prayer to the Great Spirit. Return the stones to a natural environment. Return to camp, and write in your journal and share with your partner.

✦ ✦ ✦ ✦ ✦ WORKSHEET ✦ ✦ ✦ ✦ ✦

What emotions and thoughts came up during your ceremony?

What medicine or signs happened during the ceremony, e.g., a crow flying over, traveling west to east, etc.?

WITNESS

Live in your sacred witness. That inner place of silence and observing is your true identity and therefore your true power. It is all you really have when all else is gone. Like monoliths in an ancient valley, the great stones observe and remember the passage of the ages. The answers that you find through the timelessness of spirituality and the innocence of nature offer the infinite. Each human being is on his or her own path each different from yours. Answers to your questions are rarely found in another human. Answer your own questions by reflecting on nature and conversing with your own sacred witness. Rocks like the Pyramids or the stones on Easter Island are a testimony to time gone by, to the oceans of consciousness and unconsciousness that have existed before us. The stone monuments also represent the human in the passage of time and the universality of truth that is held within Mother Earth. It is important to learn to stand still, in silence, in the sacred witness within you. Meditate on stones and the great rock formations that have lived through the ages. Move into the essence of those stones. Through the stillness you become aware of, you will begin to experience the sacred witness that lives inside you. Listen to your heart, because the sacred witness is, in the end, all that you have, but it takes great wisdom and illumination to become your sacred witness.

—The Power Deck

REBIRTH OF THE SELF-LODGE

❖ ❖ ❖ ❖ ❖ ❖ ❖ ❖ ❖ ❖ ❖ ❖ ❖ ❖ ❖ ❖

Introduction

Menopause is a time of celebration. The main teaching of the sacred gourd is to celebrate what you have become. Then you give rebirth to yourself within your gourdlike womb through celebration and ceremony. *Celebration* is an interesting word, because it implies that you are alive and existing totally and completely within the moment. To celebrate what you have accomplished in your life, to celebrate who you are, what the meaning of your life is, is to stand in the moment, in the center, equidistant from all positions on the perimeter of your sacred circle and proclaim to the world that you are something special, that you have survived in a way that has promoted your life and the life of others. Just simply to have lived through the past few decades is a statement of your power, your ingenuity, and your integrity. We are living through difficult times, times that stress us beyond what my teachers say that human beings should experience. We are, all of us, extraordinary powerful beings who through our love for the goodness of the universe and the light that lives within each of us have survived. And we should be ultimately proud of that extraordinary accomplishment. We are indeed warriors and warrioresses of the twentieth century, shamans in the making, building our way toward enlightenment and new fields of energy and the perfection of play.

Since celebration is such an integral part of this teaching, I would like to spend some time talking about the act of celebration, how, for instance, you celebrate your life in reality. How do you accomplish such a feat? Perhaps this is an idea that is new to you. So many people that I speak with talk about becoming, talk about healing, talk about recovering. But they have never seemingly become what they speak of. They never seemingly have healed themselves and never seemingly have they recovered. Understandably so, because in a lot of ways, we never get to a position where we feel totally complete, because life is a process of learning, of presenting new mirrors to ourselves and others so we can facilitate growth. Nevertheless, there are plateaus within that process of learning. The gateway of menopause marks one of those plateaus, because of the sacred gateways opening last year, because of what people describe as the Kaliugas in India, what the native people have described as prophecies that have unfolded throughout the history of time, this is in turn a period of history where energy is shifting and opening. But because so few of us have teachers who describe energy as a process of life, we are unfamiliar with these ideas. To us, so many of us, life is just life. The moment we are born, we forget who we really are. We forget that we come here onto this earth walk to become enlightened, that life is a process toward the ultimate light. It is the growth of a great seed that is planted. Your life is an extraordinary tree, the flowering of which, my teachers have told me, is really the process of death. You cannot live without one eye toward the goal of this life, which is death indeed. Death is the opening and the ushering of your spirit into the greater mystery, which makes all of life understandable, but to get to that point there are plateaus, as I have said. These plateaus are celebrations for what you have become, your sacred lodge of the self.

I'm going to help you build a new way of seeing this sacred lodge of the self so that you will see the play of celebration in a different and new way. As I have often told you, when I begin to work with one of you as an apprentice, I envision you as a sacred lodge, and I see the foundation of that lodge being your practical, pragmatic entry into the world—how you take care of your children, how you take care of your own body, your relationship to money, your relationship to your career, how you deal with that career and those aspects of your life that build the platform, the foundation for your sacred lodge. The dome of the sacred lodge or your higher ceremonies are only safe and effective to do when the foundation is rooted in bedrock.

Ceremony/Meditation

Take a deep breath. Close your eyes and get comfortable. Forget about your body as best you can and allow yourself to move into the sacred dreamtime with me. Take another deep breath. Relax your body, starting with your feet, feeling the energy of Mother Earth in the bottoms of your feet. Feel yourself relaxing your toes and your ankles. Take another deep breath as you release the muscles in your calves, in your thighs, in your knees. Consciously allow yourself to move more deeply into trance, relaxing all the muscles in your hips, in your stomach, and in your chest. Take another deep breath. Completely and totally relax the muscles in your fingers, in your arms, in your shoulders. Do not forget the muscles that are along your spine. Take another deep breath. Relax all the muscles between your shoulder blades and the back of your neck. Swallowing once hard, relax the muscles in your throat, the muscles around your mouth and around your eyes and your forehead, in your scalp. Take another deep breath, and breathe out your problems and your troubles, any ideas that have been dominating your day. Allow yourself to move into the center of the words I speak.

Each of you has a different idea of what sacredness is in your life. Shamanism does not ask you to believe in anything but yourself. The power of yourself. I would like you to see that there is a spirit lodge that is actually who you are. How you envision that spirit lodge is very much up to you. But the spirit lodge is a structure. It is a spiritual architecture, one stone or aspect of your character laid upon another with foundations deeply rooted into the earth so they can dispel any kind of shock, earthquake, winds, or disaster that may befall us. This is a house that is you. In essence, your feet stand squarely on the ground and your body reaches out as an antenna toward Father Sky. You interpret and you are the translator of the energies of the universe and the dimensions that surround you. So give yourself a few moments now to envision what you would call a sacred lodge, be it a sweat lodge, a log house, a skyscraper, or a temple, but it is something that is made out of strong material, unlike a teepee. It is made of substance. It is important for this visualization to see it as such. It is not a temporary dwelling. So I would like you to see this lodge in some part of the world that you feel powerful in, whether it be the desert or the wilderness or the mountains or a city. Your lodge could be a penthouse at the top of a skyscraper. Your lodge could be a log house facing the Teton Mountains in Jackson Hole, Wyoming. You could have a rock house. It could be built of stone or brick or logs or boards. But it is solid and impervious to the elements.

I'd like you to take several minutes now and traverse the world and find a place, a wilderness place. If you cannot exactly see it in your mind's eye, feel it and sense it. Remember places where you have been in your life that have filled you with power and joy and a sense of well-being.

Take some time.

Now that you have found your place, a location for this spirit lodge, I would like you now to go with me, work with me as we begin to build this spirit lodge from the ground up.

And so, you walk around the area where your spirit lodge will stand, and you touch the ground with your hands. You will dig out a foundation, a place to lay cement and building blocks down into Mother Earth. And you pray at this location. You ask for guidance, for strength to see clearly how this lodge should be built, and then dig the foundations.

I'll give you several minutes.

You have dug the foundation of your spirit lodge, there is something from your own experience and spirit that must go into the mortar, into the building of your foundation. One of the most important things in making the foundation of your spirit lodge is to place with it an acknowledgment from yourself that you have indeed accomplished something very important in life. Now this is a hard question for some of you, but what is the most important thing that you have accomplished? If I were asked that question, I would probably say that my most important accomplishment was the writing of *Medicine Woman*, because within that accomplishment, I healed the conditionings of my childhood. It was very important to me in my progress in life, even though many people might not see it that way. This is only for you. It's what you feel, what you have accomplished, big or small, but what you are proud of. So take several minutes. Figure out what you are most proud of in your life, and this may seem like a very small thing to some people. Maybe it is just overcoming some fear, but to you, that is a big deal.

So take some time, and then I will tell you what to do with that accomplishment.

Now that you have discovered your accomplishment, I would like you to place a piece of paper with your accomplishment written on it. See it, now, in your mind's eye as you write it on a piece of paper. Fold it and place it in a little medicine pouch made of red material. Tie it together with a prayer for thanks that you had the strength and the courage for this accomplishment, and place it into the foundation. Now take several minutes, if you will, and see yourself finishing the foundation on your spirit lodge.

I'll give you a few minutes.

The foundation of your spirit lodge is built. Now you need to build the superstructure, the framework, the framing of your beautiful lodge. This framework represents the skeleton of your body and the things that you have accomplished in your life that make you posi-

tive, that give you a point of view. I would like you to consider, What
is your point of view in your life? Where are you coming from in
your life process? Just to give you an example, I come from a place of
sacredness. I come from a place of belief in the power of woman. I
come from a place of healing in a sacred way.

Take a moment.

As you find different aspects that represent your point of view, take
your hammer and your nails. Pray with intent as you are framing
your spirit lodge. You are working very fast, because remember you
are working in a magical dimension, and you take a nail for each
aspect of your point of view, and you pray and you thank the Great
Spirit for your ability to have these thoughts and these attributes.
You nail them into the framework of your spirit lodge. Let there be
seven nails and seven attributes.

I'll give you some time.

Now that you have created your framework, you're going to put
on the roof of this beautiful lodge. The roof is created out of strong
materials that will keep you dry, cool in the summer and warm in the
winter. These materials reflect the light and yet protect you from
harm. How do you protect yourself from harm? I protect myself
through my own vulnerability, through deep study into the work that
I do. I know my subject, and I know it well. I know how to live.

I will give you time, now, to discover how you protect yourself
from harm. These are hard questions, and I am going to give you
extra time, and when you find how you protect yourself, take these
ideas, these parts of yourself, and invest them into the roof of your

spirit lodge. If it is tile, take a tile, and as you cement it down, cement it with prayers and thanks, with aspects of truth that represent your ability to protect yourself. Invest these prayers into the nails, into the glue, into the roofing material itself.

I'll give you some time.

Now that you have created a magnificent roof, the interior structure of your house is next. First of all, the windows will be framed and placed in. These windows are invisible, aren't they? You see through them. One of the first things that a magician learns is to be invisible. We are sorcerers of the light, not of the darkness. A dark sorcerer is invisible because he does not want to be seen doing his dirty work. We are invisible at times because we are building our strength and our power to enhance the life that we live. How do you enhance your life? What invisible aspects of your character do you treasure that sometimes you keep very private and to yourself? When you find these elements, place them with prayers in the caulking around the windows.

Take some time.

You have placed the windows, and we are now going to run the wiring and the plumbing through the walls and the floors. The plumbing and the wiring are arteries of communication, ways of tracking energy from one end of the house to another. How do you communicate? What are aspects of your communication that you are proud of? For me, those ways are the ability to write, a craft that I have studied long and hard. I have learned how to communicate my feelings and the extraordinary truths that the Sisterhood of the Shields has imparted to me. If I were to be laying the electricity and the plumbing in my sacred lodge, that's what I would be proud of. As you lay the plumbing and the electrical, place your prayers, giving thanks to those aspects of communication within yourself.

Take some time.

Now that the electrical and plumbing has been laid, we are going to put in insulation. In the insulation is the way that you feel safe in the world. For me, I wrapped myself in a knowing, not in knowledge that is acquired, usually borrowed from others, but a knowing that comes from experience of the truth. I know what I know and I know who I am. And I am proud of that. And I want you to be proud of yourselves as well. So what is it that you are proud of, that you hold close to keep you warm at night? Place prayers with those words into the insulation of your sacred lodge.

I'll give you time.

Now we are going to put up the walls, covering the insulation and the wiring and the plumbing, and these walls are a celebration of your aesthetics. They represent your understanding of beauty, of art and poetry and light. What aspects of art or poetry or music or literature do you enjoy? What means something to you? What do you turn to when you want to make yourself feel better? That's an ability. You know enough about yourself to know where to turn. You have alternatives, ways of healing yourself. Find those things and place them into the walls of your sacred dwelling.

Take some time.

We now will be putting in the floor of your sacred house. The floor is what you walk on. The floor in a sense represents what you stand for in the world. What do you stand for in the world? What are you proud of? This is your statement in life. For me, of course, it's being a shaman and an author. You may be many different things or one, but whatever it is, it is something that you feel like celebrating.

Take some time, and when you find those elements, place them in the floor with your hand and footprints in the sacred design that you walk upon in your sacred lodge.

Take some time.

Now that your floor has been laid, look up to the ceiling. Maybe you are going to leave the beams that are there. Maybe you are going to lower the ceiling. Maybe you are going to paint a mosaic, frescoes. Whatever you do to your ceiling, do it now, because it represents that part of your sacred lodge that is closest to the heavens, to the sacred, to Father Sky, to your Great Spirit. What is maybe a secret thing, the finest thing, the most unselfish thing that you have ever done in your life? Place that memory proudly into your ceiling.

Take some time.

Now you are going to landscape around your sacred lodge. Perhaps you would like to leave your landscape natural. Maybe you don't want people to see your sacred lodge, so you plant high trees and place boulders around the perimeter. Maybe you have placed your sacred lodge in such a way that nobody can see it. If you are going to landscape, landscape now and discover within yourself whether your sacredness needs to be hidden to be comfortable, or are you comfortable expressing it openly into the world? Are you afraid that people will call you weird? That you are different or separate from others? Whatever that is, acknowledge it and be proud of it. It's all right, whatever that is. This is not a place of judgment. This is a place of what is; it's a celebration of what is, and take great joy in that experience.

So, now landscape, placing your prayers into the plants and the stones and the trees.

Take some time.

Now that you have landscaped around your property, you are going to furnish your sacred lodge with everything that you need to do your sacred work. You are going to put in furniture. You are maybe going to lay rugs. You are going to put inspirational paintings on the walls, and certainly, you are going to have a bed, someplace where you can rest and dream, and a desk, and probably a fireplace. Make this as comfortable and as magnificent as you like, or decorate it sparsely, whatever fits your needs and your enjoyment. Celebration is about enjoyment.

So as you move around your lodge, be aware of whether, perhaps, you feel you don't deserve luxurious surroundings. Or are you celebrating a beautiful, exquisite place of careful beauty and thought?

Take some time. Place your prayers into the way that you arrange your sacred lodge.

And now that you are finished with your magnificent temple, I would like you to take a deep breath, and thinking back over all of the things that you have placed into this structure, what is the essence, now, of your celebration, of all of the things you have thought of? What accomplishment in your lifetime are you absolutely most proud of? Take several moments.

And now that you have discovered that one element, I'd like you to see yourself carving the words on a piece of wood. Place it over the doorway. Maybe your greatest accomplishment is conquering the fear of death. Whatever it is, see yourself carving it now and placing it over the doorway of your lodge.

Take some time.

You stand back from your lodge and you see that you have a magnificent workplace, a studio, a temple, a place of celebration. You know some would say that this is a place of worship, but remember that when you talk about worship, you are talking about something that you want to become, something outside of yourself, perhaps something that has crystallized into a form. That is not what we are after here. We are here to understand celebration. So this is not a place of worship, at least not at this juncture, but a place that stands as a statement of what you have accomplished in your life. No matter how little, no matter how grand, it is something to be proud of, because you have been given the gift of life, and life in itself is a miraculous celebration of joy.

So take a moment now to infuse life into your sacred lodge. Put flowers in it. Make it clean and sparkling. This is the lodge of your sacred self—make it beautiful.

Take several moments.

Take a deep breath, and say to yourself that you will remember all of the aspects, the building blocks, that have created your sacred lodge and the rebirth of yourself. Taking another deep breath, you come slowly out of the faraway. And you come back into the room feeling stronger, happy, full of a new knowledge about who you are and what you stand for.

Take up your journal and write down the elements you discovered.

Describe what your self-lodge looked like before it was reconstructed and after it was reconstructed.

How do you feel about your place of power—the location of your lodge?

What is the weakest place in your self-lodge?

What is the strongest place in your self-lodge?

I Am Full

Someone once said, Great Spirit, that the only thing to fear is fear
   itself.
Perhaps there is great wisdom in that comment,
Because I see all around me,
The manifestations of fear.
I see disease,
Unknown diseases running rampant.

Oh, Great Spirit, help us to heal our spirits
So that we can heal our health.
Health is the greatest gift you have given us.

As I look at the mountains reflecting the setting sun,
I see the preparation for darkness,
I see the great canyons losing their light,
Moving into a time of hibernation.
This could represent a long dark night of the soul.

But the sun will rise in the morning and new light will be brought to
   those corners
Where shadows lurk and fears abide,
And suddenly, like ghosts in the night,
They are gone, and there is a new day.

Thank you, Great Spirit, for giving us a new day.
Thank you, Great Spirit,

For bringing the sun
And illuminating the mountains of endeavor in our lives.

Each of us has a sacred mountain within us, Great Spirit,
And I am climbing, ever climbing, toward the top.
Help me on my journey, Great Spirit,
So that one day I can look out across the vast desert
From a new perspective
And see the magnificent mystery of life
As a truly reclaimed dimension of truth.

Great Spirit, You have sent so many shamans to teach us
And these shamans stand quiet, in silence,
All around the world,
In the great trees that provide such magnificent shade
From the heat of summer.

The sentinels of saguaro cactus that guard over the history of the
    land
They remember so much that we have forgotten.
Thank you, Great Spirit, for the shamans,
The great stones that create our mountains.

Thank you Great Spirit for helping me to climb, for giving me the
    will to search out what is real and true.
You are never ending in your support of me,
And I feel your hand, Great Spirit, resting at my back,
Holding me up when I would fall,

Giving me comfort

When I feel the terrors of the night encroaching.

Help me, Great Spirit, to see now across the world from my moun-

    tain peak.

Help me to see with new eyes.

Help me to hear your words whispered on the winds.

I know that you send me many allies, Great Spirit.

These allies surround me,

If only I could see them and sense their presence.

I celebrate you, Great Spirit, every day of my life,

And I give thanks

For the creation of this great schoolhouse called earth.

And I thank you for my shaman path,

For the light of the sun,

The dance of the moonlight across my path,

The stars that lend us their wisdom,

The Pleiades that give us comfort

In the teachings of ancient ones.

The buffalo roamed here once, free and stout and strong.

They have transformed now into other places in the universe,

But they have left their memory,

The sound of their hooves

As they would run in herds with the wind.

We, too, run in herds with the wind.

. . .

And Great Spirit, forgive us for not understanding the trail,
Forgive us for our ignorance
But we will do better,
And we are learning,
And we are committed to the path of heart.

Thank you, Great Spirit, for all that you have given us.
Ho!

✧ CLOSING THOUGHTS ✧

No woman stands in a place of power without reason. She can develop her awareness by examining everything closely. Looked at properly an object will cry out to you. When you know enough, you will know much about a person by the way that she picks up a glass or a pencil. You can see a thousand things in action. You can know all about a huntress by the ways she builds a fire, just as you can know about a bird by the way it builds its nest. When you look at an object or a person of power, you can see how much of a center it has. A true power object, for instance, has a center. You are drawn to these things and you don't even know why, just as the world will be drawn to you more and more as you begin to collect your power and stand in the center of your own circle. This workbook is about learning to be a woman of power.

A long time ago when I first met Agnes Whistling Elk, we were sitting by a stream in the far north of Canada near her cabin, and I was asking her about the sun, and the moon, and the stars of the Pleiades, and their place in my life and what they meant. There were a lot of things that I was very confused about. I didn't understand my passages that I had been through as a young girl. I had not celebrated them. I didn't understand the power in ceremony and the need for honoring myself. I was so in need of a teacher to point my way, and for years I could not find one. And that is the real reason why I have brought this workbook to you as a gift. These teachings were first given to me by the Sisterhood of the Shields, and I am very honored to have been able to share them with you now. As I remember back to that day when Agnes and I sat by that stream, I remember the words that she said to me so well because they moved into my heart and changed me forever. Agnes was looking at the passing water of the stream and she began to speak very quietly. "As we women are related to the water," she said, "it is good to be near moving water during your moon. We are born of the first words of the first mother, and we are of the void and we carry the void. Our blood is her body. It is sacred. It is said she was born of the water and the earth, and that is why your blood shall return to the earth and your spirit to the waters of the sacred dream. Her power shall be honored over all the earth, and all men shall know her as the beginning.

"Now that you have transformed your body into the womb-time, take care that your blood seed of our first mother is welcomed in a sacred way, for it is of her body. Her flesh has been burned that you may be given life. Her smoke will bring wisdom to your way. Smoke is a gift from the first mother's heart. Bless her memory, for she lives within you. When you eat, it is she who eats. When you smoke, it is she who takes your message to the faraway. When you bleed, it is she who bleeds. When you give your body to be divided in love, let all parts of you be in her name, so that her love can be complete on this great earth. Honor your Great Mother all the days of your life." I have never forgotten those words Agnes said to me. "It is time," she said, "that you learn about the sacred rites of feminine passage as it has been memorized and passed down through the ages by the Sisterhood of the Shields. I will begin to walk you in the sacred circle of life, and we will move back in time to the passages you went through as a young girl, and move you forward through the sacred plateaus of feminine existence."

Agnes taught me well through these many years, and as she continues to guide me, I will continue to share these teachings with you, as it seems appropriate. As I have said, the gateway of menopause and Woman at the Edge of Two Worlds marks the beginning of true Sisterhood. That has been deeply true for me, as I feel a tremendous sense of kinship with all of you, my sisters. We are, together, moving into a new dawn of history on this earth. A heightened infusion of awareness is occurring, and I truly feel that part of the power that men and women are experiencing is because all of us are taking our strength and reinventing identity in the passage of wise-blood.

✧ TASKS ✧

Meditate with your gourd, looking into the mirror, saying, "I am, I am" for five minutes.

The next day, repeat "Who am I? Who am I?" for five minutes.

The following day, stare into the mirror until your image begins to disappear. It is at that moment that you merge with the Great Spirit and the powers of creation. Do this as long as you want.

Sit with your gourd in your lap, your back against a tree if you have one, and gaze into the mirror that is inside your gourd. Discuss with Gourd Woman your point of view in life. What do you stand for? What is your truth? How do you express it in the world?

Making Your Changing Woman Doll

The Changing Woman Doll is a power doll for your altar and represents how you use power in the world. This power includes and balances both the dark and the light sides of your energy.

The Changing Woman Doll is a doll made of your power. She often carries lightning in her left hand, which represents your acts of power and celebration during your life and especially during menopause. Each part of her embodies an aspect of your power.

LEFT SIDE—Female/mother

RIGHT SIDE—Male/father

HEAD—Your spirit

HAIR—Your sacredness in the world

CORE/BACKBONE—The "killer" within you, the part that fights for you

FEET—Connection to Mother Earth; grounding

This doll holds the power of "Don't mess with me!" in her gourd tied at her waist.

She is Changing Woman. Much of her should represent what you are leaving behind. Her filling, her color, etc., can represent the power you are taking in your second life. She embodies your hopes and fears. She stands for your anger, joy, and all aspects of your being. When you look at her, there is no avoiding what you are feeling at this sacred gateway of life.

✧ DIARY ✧

Track your "moon," or menses, history. Where were you when "first blood" happened? Were you frightened? Did you fully understand the process?

Remember how you felt in those early days of your life, and make a list of the emotions that come up. Then, if possible, discover the emotions your mother was experiencing during her pregnancy with you. What were your birth and your mother's pregnancy like? What were the headlines on your birthday? What was the political, economic, and spiritual climate in those days?

Were you conceived through love or stress? All of these factors are early building blocks for your spirit-lodge of self. Strong, well-formed foundations help you to be secure in your life. If there are weak places in your foundations, identify them and replace them with new resolved and healthy forms.

Let go of old memories that cause you pain and only bring down your self-esteem. Menopause is the time to let go of what no longer brings you personal power and health. List what you are letting go of.

Take a long look at your adolescence, and then list the emotions
that you felt during that time. Then list how many of those feelings
have changed. You will find that much of your diary has to do with
your emotions, because your feelings and the phases of your moon
are intimately related to hormones and their fluctuations within your
body.

How do you feel about your body now? In your forties? In your
thirties? In your twenties? During adolescence? Earlier?

Has sexuality been important to you? Describe your ideas about menopause and sex.

How does spirit live in your body?

Meditate on your body and how you see yourself. Do you feel ashamed of your body or proud? How do you care for your body? Moving into wise-blood also means moving into exercise for the rest of your life. Exercise is essential to keep up your metabolism and for keeping your bones healthy. For all of the expanded spiritual awareness that you will be experiencing through this gateway, an equal amount of physical practice is essential to maintain your balance of spirit and health. Please take the time to outline your workout schedule here:

If you don't already, learn to live like an arrow and not like a target. Don't wait for life to happen to you. Define who you are, what your boundaries are, and where you are going.

For the last ten years, I've been describing my learning and my path. It has been a joy to do this. In continuing my journey, I would be grateful if you would share your insights with me.

Please write to me at:

Lynn Andrews
2934½ Beverly Glen Circle
Box 378
Los Angeles, CA 90077
1-800-549-0033

Please send me your name and address so I can share any new information with you.